SONG OF THE
DARK MAN

"*Song of the Dark Man* is a very personal book about a spirit, a spirit esteemed by witches and magicians. The first part looks at the folklore of the Dark Man from Irish folkloric sources as well as witch trial documents, which provide the setting and root the entity in times past. In the second part, Darragh speaks to working magical practitioners about their experiences—abstract, concrete, protective, initiatory, and sometimes terrifying—with the Lord of the Crossroads. In these encounters, visions, and ritual meetings, we see the shapes the Man in Black takes today and the effects he has on those who meet him. A fine work, and highly recommended."

AIDAN WACHTER, AUTHOR OF
SIX WAYS: APPROACHES AND ENTRIES FOR PRACTICAL MAGIC

"Who is the Dark Man? Trickster, initiator, embodiment of mystery? In this fascinating book, Darragh Mason traces the footprints of this elusive specter through folklore, history, and myth. Bringing a wide-ranging perspective together with the reporting of contemporary practitioners, *Song of the Dark Man* provides a unique focus on this liminal and eternal figure."

PHIL HINE, AUTHOR OF
CONDENSED CHAOS AND QUEERYING OCCULTURES

"Mason's *Song of the Dark Man* is a great introduction to an important aspect of contemporary occulturation: when there's a need for it (and there certainly is today), the forces of nature will take on mythological form to make us more aware of problematic issues. Specifically contextualizing the 'Dark Man' archetype in many of its fascinating forms and impacts, this book also allows magical practitioners of renown to share their own experiences of this primordial intelligence growing and eventually blooming within their psyches."

CARL ABRAHAMSSON, FILMMAKER,
PHOTOGRAPHER, MUSICIAN, AND AUTHOR OF
ANTON LAVEY AND THE CHURCH OF SATAN

"Frankly, my mind is blown. *Song of the Dark Man* is a book I wish had come out ages ago. In the years to come, I am certain Darragh will be showered with praise for this indispensable exploration of an underexamined pattern in our folklore; he deserves every ounce of it."

JOSHUA CUTCHIN, SPEAKER AND
AUTHOR OF *ECOLOGY OF SOULS*

"Darragh dares to spotlight the ineffable and creates the improbable. *Song of the Dark Man* is a captivating book that seeks to shed light on a figure I'd wager each and every one of us who draws breath has encountered at least once in our lives. For those of us who remember, like Darragh does, he deftly delves into the roots and rhizomes of numerous folklores and nightmares. Until now, any real examination of this figure has been nonexistent. I believe it's safe to say that the Dark Man has finally been given his due."

DOUGLAS BATCHELOR, HOST OF THE
WHAT MAGIC IS THIS? PODCAST

"While it is often very difficult to cover such nebulous subjects, Darragh Mason has more than succeeded. Through his meticulous research, Darragh has brought one of the most enigmatic figures back to life. *Song of the Dark Man* proves that while some entities are calcified within mythopoeic thought, others are merely waiting to be incarnated once more."

NATHANIEL J. GILLIS, LECTURER,
RELIGIOUS DEMONOLOGIST, AND
AUTHOR OF *A MOMENT CALLED MAN*

"Darragh Mason draws together a rich tapestry of folkloric, historical, and cultural materials relating to the 'Dark Man' of the Witches' Sabbath. . . . A must-read for anyone interested in the intersections of culture, experience, and the other."

JACK HUNTER, PhD., AUTHOR OF
MANIFESTING SPIRITS

SONG OF THE
DARK MAN

FATHER OF WITCHES, LORD OF THE CROSSROADS

A Sacred Planet Book

DARRAGH MASON

Destiny Books
Rochester, Vermont

Destiny Books
One Park Street
Rochester, Vermont 05767
www.DestinyBooks.com

Text stock is SFI certified

Destiny Books is a division of Inner Traditions International

Sacred Planet Books are curated by Richard Grossinger, Inner Traditions editorial board member and cofounder and former publisher of North Atlantic Books. The Sacred Planet collection, published under the umbrella of the Inner Traditions family of imprints, includes works on the themes of consciousness, cosmology, alternative medicine, dreams, climate, permaculture, alchemy, shamanic studies, oracles, astrology, crystals, hyperobjects, locutions, and subtle bodies.

Cataloging-in-Publication Data for this title is available from the Library of Congress

ISBN 978-1-64411-909-9 (print)
ISBN 978-1-64411-910-5 (ebook)

Printed and bound in the United States by Lake Book Manufacturing, LLC

The text stock is SFI certified. The Sustainable Forestry Initiative® program promotes sustainable forest management.

10 9 8 7 6 5 4 3 2 1

Text design by Virginia Scott Bowman and layout by Debbie Glogover
This book was typeset in Garamond Premier Pro with Gill Sans MT Pro, ITC Legacy Sans, Sheepman and Transat used as display typefaces

To send correspondence to the author of this book, mail a first-class letter to the author c/o Inner Traditions • Bear & Company, One Park Street, Rochester, VT 05767, and we will forward the communication, or contact the author directly at **www.darraghmason.com**.

Scan the QR code and save 25% at InnerTraditions.com. Browse over 2,000 titles on spirituality, the occult, ancient mysteries, new science, holistic health, and natural medicine.

For Mum and Dad

Contents

Acknowledgments

First and foremost, my deepest love and sincerest thanks to my partner, Michaela, without whom this book would never have been completed. Secondly, thank you to my sons for being the wonderful lights they are.

There are many people I'm indebted to in the creation of this book. Peter Mark Adams for his gentle mentorship and guidance. All the contributors who gave their time, shared their experiences and expertise with me. Thank you, Shullie H. Porter, Megan Rose, PhD, Orion Foxwood, Jessica Mitchell, David Beth, Alkistis Dimech, and Peter Grey. I give special thanks to my dear friends, the extraordinary Elise Oursa and Michelle DeVrieze, both of whom helped me beyond measure to process my own experiences and who shared their knowledge freely and with generosity.

◆ ◆ ◆

My gratitude to Richard Grossinger and the team at Inner Traditions for believing in this project and making it a reality. And thanks to Rev. Danny Nemu, Joshua Cutchin, and Patrick Huyghe.

◆ ◆ ◆

Finally, to the Dark Man for inspiration and opening the road for me . . .

Fig. 1. "The Moon" by Elise Oursa.
Image courtesy of the artist

Foreword

Peter Mark Adams

Song of the Dark Man is an important text, one that fills a notable gap in the annals of "occult" research. It provides a dedicated focus on a key, one may even say foundational, subject: the "Dark Man" of the Witches' Sabbath—a being of myth but also a shapeshifter, one who is prone to stepping out of the world of folklore and taking on an all too real presence in the lives of those who encounter him. Despite the apparent intimacy of the highly personal encounters recounted in this book, the Dark Man nevertheless manages to retain a certain archetypal quality, one that conveys an essentially cosmic rather than mundane nature, and to exert a presence whose varied manifestations span centuries across diverse cultures.

Darragh Mason is better known as an award-winning travel photographer; yet those knowledgeable concerning the breadth of his professional oeuvre will acknowledge that alongside his documentary eye for the vibrant life of cities resides a penchant for exploring those less frequented—indeed, for the most part, shunned—spaces where disease, poverty, and the lingering aftereffects of war stand as a stark reminder of that one unchanging constant: human suffering. Beyond these social concerns, however, stands a still more recondite field of interest. A fascination with those otherworldly presences who reside in a dimension tangential to our own, but one that, nevertheless, interpenetrates and impresses itself—whether for good or ill—upon our daily lives.

It should come as no surprise, therefore, to find the magnetic pull of the djinn exercising their fascination or that the photographer's lens seeks to capture their fleeting presence, one that both attracts and repels in equal measure, as they pass, unnoticed, through the interstices of our shared reality. This feature is one they share with the subject matter of the present work, the encounter with an equally puzzling, elusive, and disturbing figure: the Dark Man of the Witches' Sabbath.

This work approaches its subject matter from two, ultimately converging, perspectives. The first part provides the folkloric and witch trial sources of the Dark Man mythos, information essential for grasping the time, depth, and ubiquity of this most singular phenomena. In doing so, it leans heavily upon traditional Irish folklore, the most accessible body of material that has preserved the purity of its otherworldly, pagan vision better than almost any other source I can think of. The folklore is combined with far more detailed, we may even say intimate, accounts drawn from the sixteenth-and seventeenth-century witch trial records by way of Emma Wilby's superlative book *The Visions of Isobel Gowdie*.[1]

The second part exposes the reader to the visceral reality of contemporary encounters with the Dark Man. These accounts, related by the experiencers themselves, possess an immediacy that counterbalances the more ethereal qualities of the folklore and serves to mitigate the ideological framing that shapes not only the witch trial records, but our own rationalizing responses. A feature of these accounts is the progression evidenced in the way in which people frame their experience. Starting from entirely unexpected encounters, which remain largely opaque and inexplicable, the narrative rapidly evolves to reveal contexts wherein the phenomena begin to become increasingly integrated—experientially, metaphysically, and performatively—within living esoteric traditions.

This contextualization can best be characterized, for want of a better expression, as that which is proper to an initiated view of reality.

For in the last analysis, it is only in the context of esoteric cult practice that the phenomenon gains in intelligibility, meaning, and purpose. As a result, we are afforded a unique vantage point from which to contemplate the varied vectors of the encounter, and reflect upon how—once we move past the dread occasioned by his presence—he initiates a profoundly healing and spiritually evolutionary trajectory for each of the contacted. That being said, the identity of the being at the center of these varying manifestations remains, as ever, inscrutable, indefinable, and unyieldingly "other."

Whether he manifests as a man of normal height or standing nine feet tall, whether arriving riding a dark horse or as a dark angel, whether in silence, with a stern commanding voice or one reminiscent of all of the men of one's ancestral lineage—none of these descriptions can even begin to exhaust the range of appearances with which he chooses to manifest. Even his features remain indescribable, being reminiscent of the infinite expanse of the cosmos rather than any that are familiar to us. A primordial shapeshifter, he may appear in any one of his many theriomorphic forms, a man with cloven hooves, as a crow, a dog, or a deer. Such is the diversity of his attested forms that they lead one to ask in what sense the designation "man" is even warranted. Perhaps it is just the symbolic form that the "other" adopts as one means of communing with us? For there is about the Dark Man something irreducibly alien. We are bound to the surface of his manifold presentations—the where, when, and how that he chooses to manifest rather than the essence of who or what he is. We also emerge with a distinct sense of his being, at once both a part of and yet remote from this world, existing astride many worlds and dimensions.

One of the signal problems in reacting to these accounts, therefore, is their questionable ontological status. If taken literally, how do we account for their fantastic elements; and if they are classed as oneiric, merely reports of vivid dreams or entheogen-induced visions, how do we account for their uniformity and consistency over the course of centuries and across diverse cultures?

NIGHT JOURNEYS

Looking back through the ethnographic record, we can discern universal patterns of communal ritual that served to mediate the relationship between the numinous and the phenomenal. The oldest and most widely practiced human spiritual activity appears to have been possession trance, the rites of which we can find traces in every culture and strata of human development, from the cave walls of Paleolithic times to the early-modern agrarian communities who continued to cultivate their relationship with otherworldly overseers.

One of the earliest accounts of a community performing nocturnal "duties" under the supervision of an otherworldly overseer can be found in the writings of the Byzantine court official and historian Procopius, circa the mid-sixth century CE. In his "Gothic War", Procopius recounts[2] a curious tale concerning the men of a fishing village on the coast of Brittany. We are told that the men were "called" from their sleep late at night by a disembodied voice to ferry the souls of the dead. They found unfamiliar boats waiting for them. Although the vessels appeared empty, they were, nevertheless, sunk to the waterline, laden with the weight of the invisible souls aboard. In mere hours, they made a trip that would otherwise take a day or more. Upon arrival, the souls were called forth by another anonymous voice, freeing the men to return home.

Procopius's account helps to clarify a number of relevant issues. First, that in the pre-Christian era, traditional pagan communities readily accommodated the idea of invisible overseers cooperating in the performance of important communal offices: protection, fertility and dealing with the dead. Second, such otherworldly connections appear to have formed a traditional, that's to say, accepted and ongoing feature of communal life. Third, the nocturnal forays were recognized as possessing an ambiguous ontological status; the villagers' own account acknowledged the discrepancies between their normative perceptions and those attending their night journeys. Carlo Ginzburg's classic elucidation[3] of the witch trial records from seventeenth-century Italy, although set one thousand years later, serve to confirm the continuity of parallel traditions over time. Agrarian community groups (known, in this case, as the "Benandanti," or "good walkers") played a protective role in their nocturnal battles with "witches" in order to safeguard their community and crops. The battles, however, involved such fantastic elements that they can only be explained as being possessed of an otherworldly provenance. They certainly didn't occur on the same plane as the normative, day-to-day life of the village. We can therefore view the attested performance of such nocturnal duties, continuing over the course of a thousand years, as routine features of the life of European communities, at least up to the early modern period. This background does not, however, help to explain their more "Fortean" elements.

ETHNOGRAPHIES OF THE INVISIBLE

One of the significant changes in ethnographic practice in the last decade or so has been the increasing acknowledgment of the inexplicable, indeed fantastic, elements experienced in the context of rituals in pre-modern societies. These accounts have all too often been glossed over in the scholarly literature; nevertheless, they remain a feature of the ethnographic—and hence, scientific—record and have remained so for almost as long as anthropology has been an academic discipline. Such is the challenge they present to consensual models of reality that it has generally been thought to be academically "safer" to simply ignore them and, hence, avoid drawing out their radical implications.

Two cases, both from professional anthropologists, merit particular attention. Edith Turner's study of a Ndembu healing ritual[4] and Bruce Grindal's study of a Sisala death divination[5] mount a challenge to reductive models of reality in a particularly vivid form (as, indeed, does Maya Deren's immersive ethnography of possession in the context of Voudon ritual[6]). Edith Turner describes the phenomenology of a ritual in which the energy induced by the ritual process surrounds the circle of attendees like an atmosphere and rises within her until it precipitates a sudden "opening" of perception.[7] At this point, she records, she could actually "see" the entity that the healing ritual was extracting from the body of the sufferer. Similarly, Bruce Grindal's uninvited witnessing of a powerful divinatory ritual involving a corpse also saw him afflicted with powerful inner waves of energy culminating in a sudden "opening," resulting in his ability to "see" the powerful energies emanating from the hands of the ritualists and onto the corpse lying on a bier. This visionary encounter culminates with the corpse rising from its bier and reeling around the ritual space, banging a drum.

What clearly emerges from these accounts is that an efficacious (as opposed to a merely theatrical) ritual context provides a potent instrument for affecting a radical shift in awareness, and that this shift opens the ritualist to the experience of another order of reality—one that is not usually accessible in waking consciousness. Unlike dreams and most visions, this reality cannot be designated as oneiric or merely subjective since it possesses the same experiential—and impactful—characteristics for all of the ritual participants, and even for those on the periphery of the ritual. For as the ethnographic record makes clear, efficacious rituals exhibit a distinctively contagious quality.

We can, therefore, position the folklore regarding the Dark Man, the fantastic elements of the witch trial records, and the equally fantastic accounts of contemporary experiencers as participating in the same transpersonal context—or more precisely, *egregore*—understood as a reality structured around and accessed via a shared symbolic iconography. Now, while this accounts for the experiences arising in ritual contexts, it does not account for those sudden, unexpected irruptions of "high strangeness" that, as attested in the accounts collected here, often occur outside of a ritual context.

Otherworldly contacts are frequently reported in zones where the flow of the earth's natural energies is affected by subterranean disruptions to rock strata and the upwelling of springs. In such locations, the earth's energies appear to swirl and pool, affecting the dynamics of one's awareness and giving rise to a phenomenon known as geopsychic or geopathic stress.[8] It is for this reason that so many sacred sites and anomalous reports can be found on or near these naturally occurring geological features. The point is that highly energized spaces, such as those encountered in ritual and at sacred sites, are capable of facilitating the shifts of awareness that provide access to otherworldly realms. The corollary here is that these circumstances also facilitate the ingress of otherworldly presences, manifesting both as communication and, though more rarely, as physical appearances that serve to underline both the existence and evident agency of those beings.

There is yet a further set of circumstances that need to be considered. From a multi-incarnational perspective, it is evident that there may well be an ancestral basis for some of these encounters, especially those that are experienced—at least initially—as otherwise utterly inexplicable. From this perspective, the contacts and commitments undertaken in previous lives remain through the vagaries of death and rebirth, though our ability to recall these facts may be impaired by the process of taking incarnation and, therefore, require a jolt for our deep memory to awaken to our higher order commitments. Indeed, swirling about this entire phenomenon is the distinct patina of ancestry and lineage, a feature sometimes referred to as the possession of "witch blood"—the inherited imprints of initiations and devotions undertaken within an ancestral line, possible over the course of centuries. For such people, ingress to the realm of ancestral cult practice may appear to be effortless. In his eleventh-century collection the "Decretum," Burchard of Worms records the testimony of a witch who describes the actual practice of slipping away to the otherworldly, transpersonal domain of the Witches' Sabbath:

> in the silence of the quiet night, when you have settled down in bed, and your husband lies in your bosom, you are able, while still in

your body, to go out through the closed doors and travel through the spaces of the world, together with others.[9]

Despite his bewildering, multiform appearances, one thing, at least, is clear: an appearance of the "Black Man" is never accidental. Rather, it serves to instigate an encounter, or, better to say, an appointment, with destiny. Whatever the experiencer's reactions to their encounter, whether they be ones of horror, bafflement or epiphany, the initiatory, psycho-spiritual import of contact cannot be denied. This is, in itself, extremely telling. For we, in modernity, have, by and large, lost the context, traditions, and knowledge within which a relationship with either a landscape, its spirit inhabitants, or a figure such as the "Black Man" can become a source of insight and strength in our own engagement with life and purposeful living. To explore the material presented in this work in depth and in thoughtful reverie is to invite a renewal of this ancient connectivity.

Drawing upon these accounts, we can affirm that if there is one consistent characteristic of an encounter with the Dark Man, it is the profound and deeply personal significance that it holds for the experiencer. It has the nature of an encounter with destiny, one that urges the experiencer toward a reevaluation of their life purpose. The accounts also highlight the fact that his interventions are purposive and never random, and that they are seemingly undertaken to awaken the experiencer to the need for renewal—for them to enact an integration of the noumenal and phenomenal aspects of reality in some specific domain of their present incarnation. This idea aligns with the ancient notion of an overseer's traditional curatorship role and of the need for those awakened to this to cooperate in its realization. At the end of the day, we are speaking about a highly personal relationship with the numinous, mediated through a figure who remains, at one and the same time, both intimate and yet infinitely remote. The Dark Man mythos both defies categorization and transcends physical and temporal boundaries. It approximates a relationship with a trickster-like being who appears to occupy a tidal zone of meaning, one that pools, surges, and abates at obtuse angles to our daily lives, but also one which, nevertheless, beckons us to assume a more responsible, less materialistic conservatorship of life and nature.

PETER MARK ADAMS
ISTANBUL

PETER MARK ADAMS is an author, poet, and essayist specializing in the ethnography of ritual, sacred landscapes, esotericism, consciousness, and healing. A philosophy graduate, Peter pursues advanced studies in iconology, iconography, Renaissance art, and material culture with the Warburg Institute's School of Advanced Studies. Peter is an associate member of the European Society for the Study of Western Esotericism (ESSWE). The author of six books, including *The Game of Saturn* and *The Power of the Healing Field*, Peter has published nonfiction with Scarlet Imprint and Inner Traditions, literary prose and poetry with Corbel Stone Press and the Bosphoros Review of Books, and reviews of both esoterica and literature appear on Paralibrum.com.

Fig. 2. "The Dark Man" by David H. Sekulla.
Image courtesy of the artist

INTRODUCTION

Folkloric Footprints of a Nameless God

To ask, "Who is the Dark Man?" is to fall at the first hurdle. Some mysteries are not meant to be solved or understood in their entirety, and to attempt to do so is a fool's errand. There's a joke about asking directions in rural Ireland, where a tourist inquires of a local man, "How do I get to X town?" only to be told, "Well I wouldn't start from here." It's frustrating advice. Asking, "Who is the Dark Man?" will lead to frustration because *who* is not the right place to start, rather, *what* is. Even then, *what* will be answered with a menagerie of metaphors and similes and contradictions.

Whatever this force is, it has many names and avatars: The Devil, Old Scratch, Master Leonard, The Black Man, The Dark Rider, The Old One, The Master, Fear Dorcha, Lord of the Witches' Sabbath, The Fear Dubh, Gwyn ap Nudd, Lucifer, The Lord of the Crossroads, The Meikle Black Man, and The Father of Witches. And it takes on many forms—it is as elusive as smoke in the wind. But there are fingerprints, echoes of its presence in the form of the Dark Man. These echoes are in the testimonies of visionaries, in the accounts of witches, and in the terrifying encounters of travelers on lonely roads, wherein a pattern emerges. Most importantly, they are in our stories, our folklore and mythology. And while the Dark Man is a global, cross-culture phenomenon, this book will mostly draw its references from a British and Irish perspective.

It is within this collection of lore that we can find the *what* or, rather, a certain shape of the what—an emanation of the what—that manifested in the wildlands of Europe, from the dark forests of its eastern borders to the lonely crossroads of the Irish hinterlands. A terrible force of nature, a laughing psychopomp from the underworld, calling for us to lie in the foul rag and bone shop of the heart, to listen to the voices of the dead and the sensual whispers of the Sidhe. *What* as a device of comprehension does have significant challenges for the human mind and its need to label and define in order to understand. It is not within our capability to comprehend the motivations and behaviors of this force. But we have clues encoded within stories and folklore to show the way to a level of understanding.

This is not an academic book, for I am not a scholar. Nor is this book a book of spells and incantations, for I am not a magical authority. This book is for the curious and the haunted. There is a veiled pattern in folklore, one that is mirrored specifically in the experiences of witches and magicians. The purpose of this book is to explore that pattern and reflect on it. Behind his many names (which I will use interchangeably throughout), the Dark Man's pattern remains present. Part one of this book will explore this in stories, the interplay of the trickster and the paranormal landscape, and then in the Scottish witch trials. Part two gives the witness statements of contemporary witches, magicians, and persons who have had the Father of Witches interject in their lives. My hope is, if you recognize the pattern in your own life, this work will help give it context. The book seeks to explore this profoundly powerful phenomena and refute the misrepresentations of a maligned ancient entity.

He upsets the order of society by empowering chaos, reminding those in power of the limits to their authority, undermining their laws, faith, and science in a sort of epistemological rewilding, and doing it with a sinister smile and perfect comic timing. He guards the cold furnace of creation, the dark womb from where all things come. When he appears during times of desperation or interrupts a nighttime journey, it is a call of initiation. If you are called, it will be astonishing and horrifying. If you persist, it will be utterly transformative. If you resist, you may be consumed.

Perhaps the question we should ask is, what do the patterns in oral and written accounts tell us? He has provided when human authorities have taken, and he has given knowledge and medicine where doctors were bereft of treatments. He reminds the traveler of the perils of the road and questions their values and attachments. He is cold, lascivious, and dangerous. He is the satyric wildness watching from the shadows in the dark woods. He rides at the head of the fairy host. He is the dark one who awakens the mystic light within, the hunter, and the light bearer.

But what of us, the witnesses, those called to witchcraft and those inspired with stories, songs, and art? The dark one imparts the most precious insight into our soul's purpose on this earth. If you listen, he will share with you an understanding of the deepest chthonic powers moving through your soul, your family line, past, present, and future. He gives agency to us all through the auguries of his children . . .

. . . the witches and the storytellers.

Finally, I ask you to read as if you are sitting by your ancestor's campfire or by your neighbor's hearth. This is a work created in the spirit of the sagas and poems sung by our forebears. The true essence of the Dark Man lies not in the quotations I've used or in a swollen bibliography. It is found instead in the spaces between poetry and the heart, and where the intellect has surrendered to the primal. It is a truth beyond language, present in the arch of a dancer's back, the newborn's first cry, and the rattling breath of death.

So sit by the fire and read. Feel the flames' warmth on your face, while the Dark Man watches from the shadows at your back.

PART I

◊ ◊ ◊

Folklore and Witchcraft

1

Fire in the Blood

Spirituality and sexuality are not your qualities, not things you possess and encompass. Rather, they possess and encompass you, since they are powerful daimons, manifestations of the Gods, and hence reach beyond you, existing in themselves.

CARL JUNG, *THE RED BOOK: LIBER NOVUS*

On the 9th of February 1855, the local people of the Exe Estuary in South Devon woke up to find a hundred miles of cloven hoof prints set in the deep snow.

It appears on Thursday last night, there was a very heavy snowfall in the neighbourhood of Exeter and the South of Devon. On the following morning the inhabitants of the above towns were surprised at discovering the footmarks of some strange and mysterious animal endowed with the power of ubiquity, as the footprints were to be seen in all kinds of unaccountable places—on the tops of houses and narrow walls, in gardens and court-yards, enclosed by high walls and pailings, as well in open fields.[1]

The phenomenon became known as the "Devil's Footprints"—an apt name, not only because of the shape of the impressions but also due to the strange and baffling nature of this hundred-mile print. The Devil is, after all, the patron of hoaxers. What or who else could have achieved this impossible undertaking? And, why would anyone have endeavored to do this in the first place? The event presents several perplexing problems. Perhaps that was the point—to induce a state of confusion by showing with clear evidence that an impossible event had occurred. It wickedly left witnesses bereft of an explanation, forced to deal with the existential fallout one cloven footprint at a time.

In the 1890s, the town of Swansea in Wales decided that its church, St. Mary's, should be rebuilt. Legend has it that a local architect applied for the job, but he was beaten by the acclaimed architect Sir Arthur Blomfield. Thrilled to have a prestigious name attached to their project, the committee accepted Blomfield's proposal. The local architect didn't take this rejection lightly. Years later, he purchased a row of cottages adjacent to the church, tore them down, and in their place erected a red brick building to house the local brewery offices. There was one notable addition: a wooden carving of a horned devil, which faced the church. The local man was reputed to have prophesied: "When your church is destroyed and burnt to the ground my devil will remain laughing."[2] St. Mary's church was destroyed in the Swansea blitz in 1941, along with much of the town, but the neighboring brewery offices remained unscathed, under the watchful eye of the smiling devil, safe in his lofty seat overlooking the blackened ruins of the church.

These modern stories of the Devil keep him in our world attendant to chaos. There are far older stories, of course, with roots reaching right down through our primal hearts and into the fecundate black void of the underworld. As John Moriarty so eloquently puts it in his book *Invoking Ireland*:

Mostly though, we've forgotten all this, but folktales remember. Folktales aren't afraid. On its way to the well at the world's end, a folktale will stop by a rock and tell you that every seventh year, at Samhain, it turns into an old woman driving a cow. On its way to Linn Feic, a folktale will sit with you under a bush and, where a bard might tell you the history of your people awake, that bush will tell you the much more serious history of your people asleep.[3]

Our folktales are remnants of the dreamtime memories of our ancestors, a memory of an age before the veil between the imagined and the material hardened over. If our folktales are our dream history, then the Dark Man has haunted our dreams since the beginning. The appearance of the Dark Man can be a call to initiation into witchcraft, a warning of some kind, or a demand to act. Most who hear him have their lives turned upside down, and only if they pass his trial will their world reconfigure into something new. This transformation is painful, challenging, or utterly illuminating, and often all those things at once. The Dark Man demands that we examine our lives. He will oppose inertia and push us abruptly toward a new life. Perhaps your dreams have been visited by him, or your way along a lonely road has been blocked by him. Maybe you've taken the initiative yourself and have gone to the crossroads to strike a bargain. Irrespective of how it happens, you will be challenged. The Witchfather is dangerous, ruthless, and may devour you. If you pass the challenge, initiation follows. If you run, things will probably get worse. I will not be so foolish as to claim to understand his deeper motivations. I can only share what has come to me and what I have experienced.

Encounters with the Dark Man tend to present in a suitable cultural and belief framework. The first time I saw the Dark Man was the most intense visionary experience of my life. It surpassed anything I had experienced before or since. It was a mix of Judeo-Christian and Western esoteric symbols, along with personal references. Given my cultural background, this is unsurprising. The experience left me stunned, fearful, and searching for answers. Eventually, with help, I was able to work through it and come to a new understanding.

The story within this book is an old one, of the dark daimon of humanity. But what of the elusive nature of creativity—where does creativity come from? Why do some access it so easily when others do not? Inspiration is often said to come from an external force, a voice looking for the right person through whom it can express itself. The very word attends to this. It's derived from the Latin *inspirare*, meaning to breathe or blow into. This external voice in the Islamic world is said to be the djinn, whose whispers were believed to inspire poetry. In Ireland, the fairies were associated with the inspiration of the greatest pipers. What of *story* and, in particular, our folklore? Wild, fanciful themes that come down to us from various lands and across vast arcs of time tend to be explained away by the ebb and flow of human migration. What if the stories told at thousands of hearths are an attempt to describe experiences beyond a reductionist understanding of the world?

Some of the greatest minds in history have described an external force and how it drove their creativity forward. Commonly, it's referred to as one's daimon. Napoleon, Jung, and Goethe all described such a force. The Greek word *daimon* describes an intermediary spirit that acts as a bridge between the individual and the otherworld. The concept varies across geographical and ideological boundaries, and is also known as the muse, the *qareen* in Islam, and the co-walker or *coimimeadh* in Gaelic countries. Assigned to us at birth, this spirit is said to accompany us throughout life and to be neither good nor evil, but capable of both. It is our guide in completing our soul's purpose. In Plato's *Apology of Socrates*, Socrates describes his relationship with his daimon during his trial for corruption in 399 BC:

> . . . you have heard me say at many times and places, is that something divine and spiritual comes to me, the very thing which Meletus ridiculed in his indictment. I have had this from my childhood; it is a sort of voice that comes to me, and when it comes it always holds me back from what I am thinking of doing, but never urges me forward. This it is which opposes my engaging in politics.[4]

Jung described being "In the Grip of the Daimon" in *Memories, Dreams and Reflections*, and was very clear where his loyalties lay: "But at least he [Socrates] has shown us the one precious thing: 'To hell with the Ego-world! Listen to the voice of your daimonion. It has a say now, not you.'"[5]

Jung's relationship with his daimon was not without its challenges. At times he found it relentless in its ambitions to the point that he felt compelled by it against his will.

> I had to obey an inner law which was imposed on me and left me no freedom of choice . . . A creative person has little power over his own life. He is not free. He is captive and driven by his daimon . . . This lack of freedom has been a great sorrow to me.[6]

The creative impulse can be experienced as a form of possession: a drive to create and expel something that insists on being birthed. Creativity is a dangerous force and, if not managed, can take a heavy toll. Daimons are indifferent to social requirements, and the artist in the grip of the daimon may travel across the conventions of society and culture. Eventually society and culture may follow the artist enthusiastically, but this tends to happen long after death. Artists are driven to explore and find the novel, and the daimon provides visions, intuition, and compulsion. The journey can be exciting and exhilarating, but it is a dangerous and lonely one; the list of casualties is long. Jung paints a stark picture of the condition:

> A person must pay dearly for the divine gift of creative fire. It is as though each of us was born with a limited store of energy. In the artist, the strongest force in his make-up, that is, his creativeness, will seize and all but monopolize this energy, leaving so little left over that nothing of value can come of it. The creative impulse can drain him of his humanity to such a degree that the personal ego can exist only on a primitive or inferior level and is driven to develop all sorts of defects—ruthlessness, selfishness ("autoeroticism"), vanity, and other infantile traits. These inferiorities are the only means by which it can maintain its vitality and prevent itself from being wholly depleted.[7]

If daimonic creativity is a double-edged sword, who wields it? The ancient force of the Dark Man expresses through the obsession of the

creative soul, whether the human vehicle is willing or not. What artist has not painted the Devil's portrait? What author has not crafted
a wicked maestro whose manipulations grease the wheels of the plot?
The Devil has all the best tunes. So embedded is he in musical lore
that the talented are sometimes tarnished with accusations of a satanic
contract as the source of their abilities. From Jimmy Page to violinist
Niccolò Paganini, the song remains the same. The most famous folklore
of musical devilry belongs to the blues. Legend has it the Dark Man
took Robert Johnson's guitar and tuned it at the crossroads and handed
it back to him along with talent, success, lovers, and money in exchange
for his soul. The legend was so pervasive that the blues itself was forever
associated with the story and earned the epithet "the music of the devil."
Johnson's impact is extraordinary, with luminaries like Keith Richards,
Robert Plant, Bob Dylan, and Eric Clapton all citing him as an influence. In an interview in the early 2000s, Dylan, asked why he was still
working after his many years of success, replied, "It all goes back to the
destiny thing. I made a bargain with it a long time ago, and I'm holding
up my end." When pressed to reveal with whom he made a deal, Dylan
gave a wry smile, laughed, and said, "With the Chief Commander of
this earth and the world we can't see."[8] Dylan's use of the phrase "Chief
Commander of this earth" is intriguing and suggests an understanding
of what the Dark Man is.

While Dylan sought him out, there are those whom *he* seeks out.
These people may already have a link to the Dark Man via their ancestral lines or previous incarnations. There are those whom he has chosen
to call to witchcraft for no obvious reason. Which brings us to the concept of witchblood. Witch and author Mat Auryn writes:

There's something different about witches, something that draws
you to other witches and to witchcraft in general. Something that
tells you who is a witch and who isn't, despite whether they pro-
claim themselves that or shy away from it. Something deeply felt
where you know and sense someone else as your own kind. It's the

unquenchable thirst for more, for connection with others and for connection to what Orion Foxwood calls the Greatest Witch of them All; the Earth. It's a predisposition to magick, to spirit communication and to psychic experiences and an ability to sense and relate to that quality within another.[9]

Blood has long been a shorthand for the birthright associated with rulership and inheritance, and ugly concepts like eugenics. Couched in this language, the term *witchblood* can suggest connotations of ownership and exclusion. This muddies the water. Witchblood is an ineffable mystery and nothing to do with what is in the veins. In his interview for this book (chapter 12), author, witch, and Elder in Traditional Craft Orion Foxwood describes the witch's relationship with witchblood and gives significant insight into the Dark Man's motivations—the continuation and proliferation of witchcraft:

> To become an awakened and embodied witch, a soul that has been a witch before must return and be born or adopted into a blood-lineage that also has witchblood in it. Often the genetic propensity of witchblood in family has been in a forced dormancy—repression caused by trauma linked to Inquisitions or other religious or social events often having deadly circumstances. They come into their current bloodline already carrying magical traits for resolving, transmuting, and healing ingrained maladaptive, toxic, abusive and otherwise harmful patterns. The ability to do this is a soul-based and/or previous genetic trait—and thus, the concept of the witchblood. The origins of it was a mating of human and otherworldly traits. This means that "the buck stops here for cross-generational trauma-curses." In exchange, the blood of the ancestral lineage releases to the witch, inherent dormant or recessed magical, subtle sensory, and healing abilities and skills. The healing they bring to the blood is internal and external and may involve otherworldly beings that are noncorporeal that may be a part of the soul's inherent allies or those

received from another witch (living or dead), the blood family, or a personal experience.

I have a saying: there are only two things every witch must know. Don't tangle up your lines, or contaminate your flow, because every witch is born to untangle the knots of the Inquisition and other events from their blood. We hid things in the bloodline, only to come back through and unpack it like a gift waiting. But there's a cost to it. The cost is that the blood gives you back something it held for you, and you bring something that the blood needed. What the blood needs is to carry the legacy of the witchblood forward.

Perhaps we can find a metaphorical description of the difference that Mat Auryn describes in folklore of the djinn and the fairies. The Qur'an states that Allah created three sapient races. The first, angels, were created from light. The second, djinn, were created from the smokeless fire of the desert wind. And the third, human beings, were formed from clay.

> The jinn out of smokeless fire.
>
> QUR'AN, 55:15

Like human beings, the djinn can be good, evil, or neutrally benevolent. Like human beings, they have free will. The Qur'an says that the ruler of the djinn, Iblis (often depicted in Islamic paintings with a black face and body) was among the angels whom God ordered to bow down to Adam after his creation:

> We said to the angels, "Bow down before Adam," and they all bowed down, but not Iblis: he was one of the jinn and he disobeyed his Lord's command. Are you [people] going to take him and his offspring as your masters instead of Me, even though they are your enemies? What a bad bargain for the evildoers!
>
> QUR'AN, 18:50

The angels had no free will, and they could only obey Allah. Iblis, however, was very clear in his contempt for Allah's new creation:

> Iblis said, "I am better than him: You made me from fire and him from clay."
>
> QUR'AN, 38:76

Despite Iblis's animosity toward humanity, folklore tells us that the djinn have had more than a passing sexual interest in humans. In Morocco, the djinn Aicha Qandisha is said to be a beautiful woman with the legs of a goat who seduces handsome young men. The American novelist and composer Paul Bowles described the scale of Aicha Qandisha's influence in his interview for *Rolling Stone* magazine in 1974. The interview took place in Tangier where Bowles had lived since 1947:

> She's legion, she's manifold. I have a book that says about 25 years ago, there were 35,000 men in Morocco married to her. A lot of people in Ber Rechid—the psychiatric hospital—are married to her.
>
> *What exactly happens if you look at her?*
>
> . . . Then you're married to her and that's that. You begin behaving very strangely. There are several well-known husbands of Aicha Qandicha around Tangier: they walk along brooks and river beds, hoping to hear her voice—you see them wandering . . .
>
> *A contagious psychosis . . .*
>
> Right. And when they find Aicha Qandicha again, they make love to her right there, doesn't matter who's there.[10]

Unsurprisingly, accounts of this nature are accompanied by stories of the children produced from encounters with amorous spirits. The Queen of Sheba herself was said to be part djinn, and djinn hybridism is an idea supported by certain hadiths.

"Among you are those who are expatriated (mugharrabûn);" and this, he explained, meant "crossed with jinn."

SUYUTI, LAQT AL-MARJÂN[11]

The same idea exists within Irish and British lore, which is unsurprising given that fairies are said to share the same interest in humans as the djinn do. In fact, folklore tells of numerous Irish families having fairy ancestors. During the Great Scottish witch hunt of 1597–1598, witch Andro Man was put on trial at the age of 70.

> Thow confessis that be the space of threttie twa yeris sensyn or thairby, thow begud to have carnall deall with that devilische spreit, the Quene of Elphen, on quhom thow begat dyveris bairnis.[12]

Andro Man confessed to having a carnal relationship with "that devilish sprite, the Queen of Elphame with whom he begat several children." This is far from an isolated case and the Dark Man, as I will explore later in this book, is a horny old goat. Perhaps the folkloric accounts of his lascivious nature are the source of his epitaph Father of Witches. While hybridism is interesting to explore, I believe it to be (mostly) a folkloric metaphor for the transformation that takes place through the Dark Man and the spirits in his pay. In British and Irish folklore the Dark Man and the fairies are inextricably linked. Perhaps, by extension, so too are witches. Born in 1798, Biddy Early was an Irish witch from County Clare, around whom there is a superb body of folklore. She was said to be a strange child who spent time alone, talking to the fairies.

> But in three hours, she wasn't back, so her mother went looking for her. And she found her above, under whitethorns, chatting and talking away. She didn't even know her mother was talking to her when she met her, she was so engrossed in it. She could see things another couldn't see.[13]

Revisiting the term *witchblood*, I personally prefer the phrase "fire in the blood." It subsumes the meaning of witchblood and invokes the illuminative qualities of inspiration and received mysticism that the Dark Man ignites in the hearts of his children. A determining sign of having fire in the blood seems to be having sensitivity to and the ability to work with the emissaries of the otherworld. Having fire in the blood does not determine proficiency or understanding, which is why it is almost universal that societies have a shamanic tradition or a mystery school where those with capabilities can train to engage with the spirit world.

The archetypal form of the Dark Man embeds itself in our stories and art through daimonic inspiration. He works more closely with witches through the mystic gifts of fire in the blood. To what end is unfathomable. The mystery has no center. There is no complete picture possible through the aperture of human experience. Witch Robin Artisson describes the Dark Man as follows:

> The secret is that he has no original or native form, no beastly body, no human form, and no godly or immortal form. That's why he's the Master Shape-Shifter, the immortal, the most clever, the living secret beyond words and ideas, beyond measures of time and vast depths of space. This is how he opens the Eye above the Eyes that sees everything; this is how he is able to be whatever he needs to be, at any given time, when the gaze of any human falls on him.[14]

Of this inspirational, disruptive force there is no singular name or form. There are no canonized religious texts. Instead there are many shared characteristics and overlapping mythologies. We are left with fragments from folklore and witchcraft, which we piece together as best we can. This task is urgent; our very survival depends on it. Our seers and cunning folk have been burned and drowned. We are at odds with the natural world. Cowed by and absorbed into orthodoxy, we've forgotten his songs. If we follow the cloven footprints in the snow, the way home will be illuminated by the fire in our blood and we will sing the song of the Dark Man again.

2

The Black Magician of the Men of God

"He is everywhere," she whispered.
"He is in the bushes, and on the hill.
He looked up at me from the water,
and he stared down on me from the sky.
His voice commands out of the spaces,
and it demands secretly in the heart.
He is not here or there,
he is in all places at all times.
I cannot escape from him," she said,
"and I am afraid."

"SADHBH ON THE DARK MAN" IN
IRISH FAIRY TALES BY JAMES STEPHENS

Grimm's fairy tales for children are anything but gentle bedtime tales to send little ones off to sleep, dreaming of knights and princesses. They are moral tales, strict lessons of the repercussions of one's conduct. Deception and avarice are punished, and honesty and kindness rewarded. Beyond the simple moral themes emerge more adult warnings. Beware the stranger and think twice before walking that lonely forest path alone.

Our mythologies and folklore are templates for the spectrum of the human experience. Some tales hold within them secret knowledge, clues to the mysteries of the world. Such tales can be found in Irish mythology in a collection known as The Fenian Cycle, a body of Irish literature originally dating from the seventh century. The Ireland of the Fenian Cycle is one in which noble warriors of the Fianna spend their time hunting, fighting, and engaging in adventures in the spirit world. The earliest compilation of Fenian stories is found in the *Acallam na Senórach* or the *Colloquy of the Ancients*. The text is made up of three manuscripts: two from the fifteenth century—*The Book of Lismore* and *Laud 610*—and a third from Killiney, County Dublin, dating from the seventeenth century. Linguistic evidence however, dates the text earlier, to the twelfth century. The manuscripts reflect a far older oral tradition of the Fenian tales and, more importantly in the context of this book, the archetypal characters in the stories. Apart from Latin, Irish is the oldest vernacular literary language in western Europe. Despite the presence of pagan culture and beliefs, the medieval Irish monks felt compelled to record their tales. This points to the deep cultural meaning these myths and poems had on the contemporary Irish identity and its interpretation of the world.

Two families, or Clans, make up the Fianna: the *Clann Baiscne*, commanded by *Fionn mac Cumhaill* (commonly transcribed as "Finn MacCool"), and the *Clann Morna*, led by his rival, *Goll mac Morna*. Fionn's father, *Cumhal*, was killed in combat by Goll, and the boy Fionn was raised in hiding. Eventually Fionn became the chief of the Fianna and various accounts of their exploits have been told. The cycle includes "The Pursuit of Diarmuid and Gráinne" and "Oisín in Tír na nóg," two of the best-known Irish tales.

Most of the poems are attributed to Fionn's son, Oisín, whose unfortunate time-traveling adventures form a narrative connecting the heroic world of the Fianna—rich with fairy women, giants, and liminal lands—to the time of St. Patrick. Eventually, early medieval Irish monks transcribed the poems into the written form, which provided an opportunity to show the authority of the Christian god over the fairies, sorcery, and heroes of pre-Christian Ireland. In the process of this documentation, they preserved the tales of the Fianna, which otherwise may have been lost in the mists of time. In the conversations between St. Patrick and Oisín it is notable that the venerable saint does not win all the debates. He is well matched by Oisín, which is interesting given Oisín's maternal heritage is not human; Oisín is half fairy. The name Oisín means *little deer* or *little fawn* as his mother, the fairy-woman Sadhbh, gave birth to him in the form of an enchanted deer. This detail could be put down to the fair-mindedness of the Irish monks or perhaps an indication of a spiritual dual practice. The roots of the story of Oisín's conception go back to the twelfth century at least. In a couple of marginal quatrains in the Book of Leinster, Oisín's mother—there called *Blái Derg*—was in the form of a deer when he was conceived.

> *Blái used to come in the shape of a doe*
> *And join the díbherg-band*
> *So that Oisín was thus begotten*
> *Of Blái Derg in the shape of a doe.*[1]

In the theme of "fairy women as a deer" we start to see a pattern through which the subject of this book begins to appear. In the later folk traditions of Scotland and Ireland, the story of Oisín's birth features a druid with a name that denoted a dark appearance and nature, An Fear Dorcha or An Fear Dubh, meaning The Dark Man or The Black Man respectively. This Dark Man was responsible for changing Oisín's mother, known in the later Irish tradition as Sadhbh, into the shape of a deer. The pattern appears again in *The Colloquy of the Ancients*, in which Caoilte mac Rónáin and the Fianna are told by the Lord of the Dead, Donn Dubh (Dark or Black Donn), on a visit to Donn's otherworld fort that he sent the Lady Máil to them in the form of a deer to lure them to his fort. In the feast that follows Donn tells them:

> . . . and we sent that maiden Máil to meet you [i.e. Caoilte] to
> Tory (Island) in the north of Ireland, in the shape of a young wild
> deer-calf, and ye followed her until ye reached this dwelling, and the

young one that ye see with the fully green mantel on her, that is her, said Donn.[2]

Here we have an underworld Lord with a name denoting darkness who uses magic to turn a fairy woman into a deer in order to deceive the warriors of the Fianna. We find the theme again in a twelfth-century poem entitled "Faffand" from *The Metrical Dindshenchas*: a series of ancient legends connected with the origin of Irish place names. These legends passed down through time orally before being put into text by medieval Irish monks. The poem recounts how a supernatural woman, Aige, was changed into a wild doe by the evil spirits:

> Broccaid the powerful with winning of hostages, of the bright
> and famous race of the Galian, he had a son, Faifne the
> poet; the record of his final madness is no falsehood.
> It was she was the mother of the comely son,—even Libir
> quick and eager of mood: their daughter was the swift
> lady of the hosts Aige, the noble and skilful.
> Exceeding fair were the four, curled and gentle; they were
> a noble kin, of virtuous behaviour, the father and the
> lovely mother, the daughter and the brother soft and fair.
> The evil spirits made an onset (it was no feeble deed of
> wanton folly):—they changed into the form of a wild doe
> the noble Aige of the love-spots.
> She traversed Erin from shore to shore fleeing before all the
> fierce and fiery packs; so that she coursed round Banba,
> land of judges, bravely, four fair times.
> Her doings and her valiance had an end, here came to pass
> her final dissolution; they tore her in pieces in their
> wickedness, did the warriors of Meilge of Imlech.[3]

The Dark Man himself shapeshifts into a deer in the famous confession of seventeenth-century Scottish witch Isobel Gowdie, who described the Devil as a "meikle blak roch man" who "somtymes he haid buitis & somtymes shoes on his foot bot still his foot ar forked and cloven he vold be somtymes w[i]th ws lyk a dear or a rae."[4] In modern English this account reads as a "great black rough man" who "sometimes would have boots or shoes on his feet but still his feet are forked and cloven" and would "sometimes be like a deer or a roe deer." Gowdie's remarkable confession provides an experiential link between folklore and witchcraft and the Father of Witches.

Later versions of Oisín's birth story feature a dark druid who casts that now familiar spell, transforming the fairy woman into a deer. To demonstrate the thematic pattern of the Dark Man, I will examine two versions of this tale. The first comes from *Celtic Myths and Legends* by T. W. Rolleston.[5]

One day, as Finn and his companions and dogs were returning from the chase to their dún on the Hill of Allen, a beautiful fawn started up on their path, and the chase swept after her, she taking the way which led to their home. Soon all the pursuers were left far behind save only Finn himself and his two hounds Bran and Skolawn. Now these hounds were of strange breed; for Tyren, sister to Murna, the mother of Finn, had been changed into a hound by the enchantment of a woman of the Fairy Folk, who loved Tyren's husband Ullan; and the two hounds of Finn were the children of Tyren, born to her in that shape. Of all hounds in Ireland they were the best, and Finn loved them much, so that it was said he wept but twice in his life, and once was for the death of Bran.

At last, as the chase went on down a valley-side, Finn saw the fawn stop and lie down, while the two hounds began to play round her, and to lick her face and limbs. So he gave commandment that none should hurt her, and she followed them to the Dan of Allen, playing with the hounds as she went.

The same night Finn awoke and saw standing by his bed the fairest woman his eyes had ever beheld. "I am Saba (Sadhbh), O Finn," she said, "and I was the fawn ye chased to-day. Because I would not give my love to the Druid of the Fairy Folk, who is named the Dark, he put that shape upon me by his sorceries, and I have borne it these three years. But a slave of his, pitying me, once revealed to me that if I could win to thy great Dún of Allen, O Finn, I should be safe from all enchantments, and my natural shape would come to me again. But I feared to be torn in pieces by thy dogs, or wounded by thy hunters, till at last I let myself be overtaken by thee alone and by Bran and Skolawn, who have the nature of man and would do me no hurt." "Have no fear, maiden," said Finn; "we, the Fianna, are free, and our guest-friends are free; there is none who shall put compulsion on you here."

So Saba dwelt with Finn, and he made her his wife; and so deep was his love for her that neither the battle nor the chase had any delight for him, and for months he never left her side. She also loved him as deeply, and their joy in each other was like that of the Immortals in the Land of Youth. But at last word came to Finn that the warships of the Northmen were in the Bay of Dublin, and he summoned his heroes to the fight; "For," said he to Saba, "the men of Erin give us tribute and hospitality to defend them from the foreigner, and it were shame to take it from them and not to give that to which we, on our side, are pledged." And he called to mind that great saying of Goll mac Morna when they were once sore, bested by a mighty host. "A man," said Goll, "lives after his life, but not after his honour."

Seven days was Finn absent, and he drove the Northmen from the shores of Erin. But on the eighth day he returned, and when he entered his dún he saw trouble in the eyes of his men, and of their fair women folk, and Saba was not on the rampart expecting his return. So he bade them tell him what had chanced, and they said:

"Whilst thou, our father and lord, wert afar off smiting the foreigner, and Saba looking ever down the pass for thy return, we saw one day as it were the likeness of thee approaching, and Bran and

Skolawn at thy heels. And we seemed also to hear the notes of the Fian hunting-call blown on the wind. Then Saba hastened to the great gate, and we could not stay her, so eager was she to rush to the phantom. But when she came near she halted and gave a loud and bitter cry, and the shape of thee smote her with a hazel wand, and lo, there was no woman there anymore, but a deer."

This passage of text contains one of the deepest mysteries encoded within the stories: the illusion of dualism. The story positions the Dark Man and Fionn as adversaries. The name Fionn means "white or fair-haired", setting up the opposition of Light versus Darkness. When the Dark Man appears as Fionn, it is allegorical to the darkness containing the light; these two forces are intertwined, and any separation is an illusion. The theme of human shape-shifting into animal forms suggests humans are not separate from the animal world and nature.

"Then those hounds chased it, and ever as it strove to reach again the gate of the dún they turned back. We all now seized what arms we could and ran out to drive away the enchanter, but when we reached the place there was nothing to be seen, only still we heard the rushing of flying feet and the baying of dogs, and one thought it came from here, and another from there, till at last the uproar died away and all was still. What we could do, O Finn, we did; Saba is gone."

After these events, the heartbroken Fionn searches Ireland for a trace of his fairy lover. He never sees her again. Instead he finds a boy with her likeness in County Sligo:

When he came to himself he was on the mountain-side on Ben Bulban, where he remained some days, searching for that green and hidden valley, which he never found again. And after a while the dogs found him; but of the hind his mother and of the Dark Druid there is no man knows the end. Finn called his name Oisin, and he became a warrior of fame, but far more famous for the songs and tales that he made; so that of all things to this day that are told of the Fianna of Erin men are wont to say: "Thus sang the bard Oisin, son of Finn."

James Stephens's book *Irish Fairy Tales*[6] features the same story but with further details. On a hunt, Fionn's dogs, Bran and Sceólan, will not attack a particular fawn, which appears tame, and Fionn decides to take the fawn back to his camp. That night, the fairy woman Sadhbh enters Fionn's room and begs for his protection from an evil magician, the *Fear Doirche* or *The Dark Man of the Shi*. She also offers Fionn her hand in marriage. Lovestruck, or perhaps under a fairy glamour, he agrees and promises to protect Sadhbh, naming the dark man as his enemy. In this version there is a variation in the spelling of Gaelic names. The folklorists who gathered these stories were often not Irish speakers and wrote down the names phonetically.

Late that night, when he was preparing for rest, the door of Fionn's chamber opened gently and a young woman came into the room. The captain stared at her, as he well might, for he had never seen or imagined to see a woman so beautiful as this was. Indeed, she was not a woman, but a young girl, and her bearing was so gently noble, her look so modestly high, that the champion dared scarcely look at her, although he could not by any means have looked away. As she stood within the doorway, smiling, and shy as a flower, beautifully timid as a fawn, the Chief communed with his heart.

"She is the Sky-woman of the Dawn," he said. "She is the light on the foam. She is white and odorous as an apple blossom. She smells of spice and honey. She is my beloved beyond the women of the world. She shall never be taken from me."

And that thought was delight and anguish to him: delight because of such sweet prospect, anguish because it was not yet realised, and might not be. As the dogs had looked at him on the chase with a look that he did not understand, so she looked at him, and in her regard there was a question that baffled him and a statement which he could not follow. He spoke to her then, mastering his heart to do it.

"I do not seem to know you," he said. "You do not know me indeed," she replied.

"It is the more wonderful," he continued gently, "for I should know every person that is here. What do you require from me?"

"I beg your protection, royal captain."

"I give that to all," he answered. "Against whom do you desire protection?"

"I am in terror of the Fear Doirche."

"The Dark Man of the Shi?"

"He is my enemy," she said.

"He is mine now," said Fionn. "Tell me your story."

"My name is Saeve [Sadhbh], and I am a woman of Faery," she commenced. "In the Shi' many men gave me their love, but I gave my love to no man of my country."

"That was not reasonable," the other chided with a blithe heart.

"I was contented," she replied, "and what we do not want we do not lack. But if my love went anywhere it went to a mortal, a man of the men of Ireland."

"By my hand," said Fionn in mortal distress, "I marvel who that man can be!"

"He is known to you," she murmured. "I lived thus in the peace of Faery, hearing often of my mortal champion, for the rumour of his great deeds had gone through the Shi', until a day came when the Black Magician of the Men of God put his eye on me, and, after that day, in whatever direction I looked I saw his eye."

She stopped at that, and the terror that was in her heart was on her face. "He is everywhere," she whispered. "He is in the bushes, and on the hill. He looked up at me from the water, and he stared down on me from the sky. His voice commands out of the spaces, and it demands secretly in the heart. He is not here or there, he is in all places at all times. I cannot escape from him," she said, "and I am afraid," and at that she wept noiselessly and stared on Fionn.

"He is my enemy," Fionn growled. "I name him as my enemy."

"You will protect me," she implored.

"Where I am let him not come," said Fionn. "I also have knowledge. I am Fionn, the son of Uail, the son of Baiscne, a man among men and a god where the gods are.

"He asked me in marriage," she continued, "but my mind was full of my own dear hero, and I refused the Dark Man."

"That was your right, and I swear by my hand that if the man you desire is alive and unmarried he shall marry you or he will answer to me for the refusal."

"He is not married," said Saeve, "and you have small control over him." The Chief frowned thoughtfully. "Except the High King and the kings I have authority in this land." "What man has authority over himself?" said Saeve.

"Do you mean that I am the man you seek?" said Fionn. "It is to yourself I gave my love," she replied. "This is good news," Fionn cried joyfully, "for the moment you came through the door I loved and desired you, and the thought that you wished for another man went into my heart like a sword." Indeed, Fionn loved Saeve as he had not loved a woman before and would never love one again. He loved her as he had never loved anything before. He could not bear to be away from her. When he saw her he did not see the world, and when he saw the world without her it was as though he saw nothing, or as if he looked on a prospect that was bleak and depressing.

Fionn meets the bewitched Sadhbh in the form of a fawn. In the safety of his fort the magic of the Dark Man is undone and she transforms back into a beautiful fairy woman, and Fionn falls deeply in love. He will never love another again as he loves Sadhbh. Unfortunately, fairy love affairs rarely end happily. Sadhbh calls the Dark Man the "Black Magician of the Men of God" ("the Men of God" is a reference to the Tuatha Dé Danann, the fairy race in Irish mythology). Fionn leaves his fort to fight off an incursion of men from Lochlann, and after the battle he returns to find Sadhbh gone. His servant explains that a figure who looked like Fionn approached the castle, and thinking it was Fionn, Sadhbh ran out to meet him. However, it was the shape-shifting Dark Man who turned her back into a deer, never to be seen again. Fionn spends years searching Ireland for her to no avail.

What can we deduce from the Dark Man's brief but potent appearances in the Fenian Cycle and subsequent folk iterations? I argue Donn Dubh is an expression of the Dark Man archetype. They are linked by appellation, trickster behavior, and, specifically, in the use of magic to transform another into a deer. Most importantly they are both connected to the Tuatha Dé Danann. The Irish scholar Dáithí ó hógáin describes Donn in *The Lore of Ireland* as follows:

> The name simply represents the adjective donn, meaning "brown" . . . In ancient times, the adjective usually signified "dark", and the character Donn is perennially associated with the shadowy realm of the dead. He is, however, also represented as an ancestor of those who die, and his name therefore seems to have been originally an epithet of the deity known as the Daghdha. Donn is referred to in several early texts. Particularly striking is a reference in the death-tale of Conaire, who is slain by three red-haired men, "sons of Donn, king of the dead at the red tower of the dead." These three are further quoted as saying, "we ride the HORSES of Donn—although we are alive, we are dead!"[7]

An Daghdha (the Dagda) is a significant figure in Irish mythology and one of the Tuatha Dé Danann. Daghdha is linked to the Dark Man by Sadhbh, when she calls him the "Black Magician of the Men of God." The *Lebor Gabála* or *The Book of Invasions*, which was written between the eighth and twelfth centuries, is a collection of poems in Gaelic intended to be a history of Ireland. It describes the Tuatha Dé Danann as follows:

> The Túatha Dé Danann were in the northern islands of the world, studying occult lore and sorcery, druidic arts and witchcraft and magical skill, until they surpassed the sages of the pagan arts. They studied occult lore and secret knowledge and diabolic arts in four cities: Falias, Gorias, Murias, and Findias.[8]

Thus we have a pattern linking the figure of the Dark Man—the Fear Dubh—back to the Túatha Dé Danann and a clear reference to their occult capabilities and knowledge; capabilities and knowledge that the Dark Man, the Father of Witches, continues to impart to this day, as we will see in part two of this book.

The reference to the northern islands is a detail worthy of further exploration. I believe this is a reference to the legendary land of Hyperborea. Often depicted as four islands in the north pole surrounding a great lodestone mountain known as Rupes Nigra, the land's magnetic qualities were believed to be the reason the compass pointed north. This belief was said to be echoed in a lost text called *Inventio Fortunata*, which was a travelogue of the northlands by a fourteenth-century English friar. Nothing of this book remains and many doubt it ever existed; however, it still influenced cartography and map design of the sixteenth and seventeenth centuries, including those of the great Dutch cartographer Gerardus Mercator.

Mercator describes the region thus:

> In the matter of the representation, we have taken it from the Travels of James Cnoyen of Bois le Duc, who quotes certain historical facts of Arthur the Briton but who gathered the most and the best information from a priest who served the King of Norway in the year of Grace 1364. He was a descendant in the fifth degree of

Fig. 3. The north polar regions as portrayed in
the 1595 Gerardus Mercator atlas.
Wikimedia Commons

those whom Arthur had sent to live in these isles; he related that, in 1360, an English minor friar of Oxford, who was a mathematician, reached these isles and then, having departed therefrom and having pushed on further by magical arts, he had described all and measured the whole by means of an astrolabe somewhat in the form here under which we have reproduced from James Cnoyen. He averred that the waters of these 4 arms of the sea were drawn towards the abyss with such violence that no wind is strong enough to bring vessels back again once they have entered; the wind there is, however, never sufficient to turn the arms of a corn mill.[9]

Mercator further described the islands in a letter of 1577 to none other than the great magus, Dr. John Dee:

> In the midst of the four countries is a Whirl-pool, into which there empty these four indrawing Seas which divide the North. And the water rushes round and descends into the Earth just as if one were pouring it through a filter funnel. It is four degrees wide on every side of the Pole, that is to say eight degrees altogether. Except that right under the Pole there lies a bare Rock in the midst of the Sea. Its circumference is almost 33 French miles, and it is all of magnetic Stone.[10]

In the Islamic world this mountain was known by another name, Qaf-kuh or Mount Qaf. It is the reputed homeland of the djinn where their great emerald jeweled cities grace its steep slopes. The mountain range is composed of green chrysolite and is said to reflect the greenish tint to the sky (which we call the northern lights). Perhaps these cities were where the Tuatha Dé Danann gained their occult mastery. Both fairies and djinn have almost identical origin myths of being expelled from heaven after rebelling against God. The principal difference is that in Irish lore, the fairies *are* the fallen angels, while the djinn are their own species.

Finally, in the apocrypha text *The book of Adam and Eve*, there are two verses strengthening the connection between the Devil, the Tuatha Dé Danann, and the mythic north. Satan says to Adam and Eve: "And it was so, that when He had created me, He placed me in a garden in the north, on the border of the world."[11] And later he said to Cain: "My relations are in a garden in the north, where I once meant to bring your father Adam; but he would not accept my offer."[12]

This raises the question of who are Satan's relations? Presumably the fallen angels, the Tuatha Dé Danann.

3

Oisín, The Little Fawn

There is no one at all in the world the way I am;
it is a pity the way I am; an old man dragging stones;
it is long the clouds are over me to-night!
I am the last of the Fianna, great Oisin, son of Finn,
listening to the voice of bells;
it is long the clouds are over me to-night!

Oisin's "Laments"

After seven years of searching for his abducted beloved, Fionn finds a young boy in the forest whom he recognizes as his and Sadhbh's child. The boy tells Fionn of his years spent in Fairyland, when the Dark Man kept him and Sadhbh, still in deer form, in a cave before finally sending the boy to the world of men.

"I used to live," he said, "in a wide, beautiful place. There were hills and valleys there, and woods and streams, but in whatever direction I went I came always to a cliff, so tall it seemed to lean against the sky, and so straight that even a goat would not have imagined to climb it."

"I do not know of any such place," Fionn mused.

"There is no such place in Ireland," said Caelte, "but in the Shi' there is such a place."

"There is in truth," said Fionn.

"I used to eat fruits and roots in the summer," the boy continued, "but in the winter food was left for me in a cave."

"Was there no one with you?" Fionn asked.

"No one but a deer that loved me, and that I loved."

"Ah me!" cried Fionn in anguish, "tell me your tale, my son."

"A dark stern man came often after us, and he used to speak with the deer. Sometimes he talked gently and softly and coaxingly, but at times again he would shout loudly and in a harsh, angry voice. But whatever way he talked the deer would draw away from him in dread, and he always left her at last furiously."

"It is the Dark Magician of the Men of God," cried Fionn despairingly.

"It is indeed, my soul," said Caelte. "The last time I saw the deer," the child continued, "the dark man was speaking to her. He spoke for a long time. He spoke gently and angrily, and gently and angrily, so that I thought he would never stop talking, but in the end he struck her with a hazel rod, so that she was forced to follow him when he went away. She was looking back at me all the time and she was crying so bitterly that any one would pity her. I tried to follow her also, but I could not move, and I cried after her too, with rage and grief, until I could see her no more and hear her no more. Then I fell on the grass, my senses went away from me, and when I awoke I was on the hill in the middle of the hounds where you found me."

That was the boy whom the Fianna called Oisin, or the Little Fawn. He grew to be a great fighter afterwards, and he was the chief maker of poems in the world. But he was not yet finished with the Shi. He was to go back into Faery when the time came, and to come thence again to tell these tales, for it was by him these tales were told.[1]

What are the motivations of the Dark Man in this tale? How do these stories serve him? Looking at the tale of Oisín's birth, we can surmise it allowed for a link through time that placed the Dark Man in the

Irish psyche. From Daghdha to Donn Dubh, to the Fear Dorcha and later to the Fear Dubh, we have a thematic chain linking versions of the tale back to twelfth-century manuscripts and further into antiquity via oral tradition.

Through this story he is established as "The Dark Magician of the Men of God," meaning the Tuatha Dé Danann. His use of a hazel wand, his shape-shifting, and his glamour magic all define him as a fairy. The transforming deer motif also links him to Donn Dubh, the Lord of the Dead. The world of the fairy and the world of the dead are often intertwined, so this is unsurprising. There is a challenge to duality within this tale of Oisín's birth. The Fear Dubh represents dark and chaos with Fionn representing light and order. The Fear Dubh's interjection into Fionn's life leads to the birth of the half fairy–half human hero-poet Oisín, and in doing so immortalizes them all in mythology. This outcome demonstrates how the seemingly separate and opposing forces of light and darkness are in fact the dance partners that create our world. The Dark Man is enfolded within the larger force of Lucifer and plays out his own part in the creative process. It is allegorical of the great mystery of creation: from the darkness comes the light. It is a mystery we see illustrated in the first chapters of the Bible.

> And the earth was without form, and void; and darkness [was] upon the face of the deep. And the Spirit of God moved upon the face of the waters. And God said, Let there be light: and there was light.[2]

This is not a linear process, but a cycle that is beyond human understanding, which is why folklore and mythology are suitable vehicles for the transmission of this concept: it is better rendered through the mythopoetic.

Oisín grew into a man and joined his father's band of heroes, making a name for himself as a great poet and warrior. Oisín's stories provided the source material of the controversial work of Scottish poet James Macpherson. His 1762 book *Fingal* centered on the hero poet

Ossian and it was extraordinarily famous across Europe. Napoleon Bonaparte himself was a devoted fan.

> In August 1797, the future Grand Master of the Imperial University, Jean-Pierre-Louis de Fontanes, wrote a letter praising the young general Bonaparte to the skies. "It is said," he enthused, "that you always have a copy of Ossian in your pocket—even in the midst of battles." The sixteen-year-old Lamartine wrote of his own coming of age in 1806, calling those years "the time when Ossian [. . .] ruled the imagination of France." The painter/art critic Etienne-Jean Delécluze, Jacques-Louis David's favourite pupil, noted in his memoirs that in the years following the First Italian Campaign it had been Bonaparte himself who spread the mania for Ossian in France.[3]

Indeed Napoleon remained an ardent fan of Ossian throughout his life, ". . . for Maitland spotted Ossian amongst Napoleon's books on Bellerophon."[4]

Ossian's star faded as evidence emerged that there was little to Macpherson's claims to have translated the poems from third-century Scots Gaelic texts, and in fact they were largely a construct of Irish Fenian mythology, Gaelic songs, and Macpherson's own creativity. The whole affair would have appealed to the Dark Man's sense of humor.

In the story "Oisín in Tir na nÓg" (Oisín in the land of the young), Oisín was hunting deer with his band of heroes on the shores of Loch Léin, County Kerry, when, from the west, a rider on a white steed emerged out of the sea mists. The rider was the fairy woman, Niamh Cinn-Óir.

> . . . they saw coming towards them a maiden, beautiful exceedingly, riding on a snow-white steed. She wore the garb of a queen; a crown of gold was on her head, and a dark-brown mantle of silk, set with stars of red gold, fell around her and trailed on the ground. Silver

shoes were on her horses hoofs, and a crest of gold nodded on his head. When she came near she said to Finn: "From very far away I have come, and now at last I have found thee, Finn son of Cumhal." Then Finn said: "What is thy land and race, maiden, and what dost thou seek from me?"

"My name," she said, "is Niamh of the Golden Hair. I am the daughter of the King of the Land of Youth, and that which has brought me here is the love of thy son Oisin." Then she turned to Oisin, and she spoke to him in the voice of one who has never asked anything but it was granted to her.

"Wilt thou go with me, Oisin, to my father's land?" And Oisin said: "That will I, and to the world's end"; for the fairy spell had so wrought upon his heart that he cared no more for any earthly thing but to have the love of Niamh of the Head of Gold. Then the maiden spoke of the Land Oversea to which she had summoned her lover, and as she spoke a dreamy stillness fell on all things, nor did a horse shake his bit, nor a hound bay, nor the least breath of wind stir in the forest trees till she had made an end. And what she said seemed sweeter and more wonderful as she spoke it than anything they could afterwards remember to have heard, but so far as they could remember it it was this:

> Delightful is the land beyond all dreams,
> Fairer than aught thine eyes have ever seen.
> There all the year the fruit is on the tree,
> And all the year the bloom is on the flower.
> There with wild honey drip the forest trees;
> The stores of wine and mead shall never fail.
> Nor pain nor sickness knows the dweller there,
> Death and decay come near him never more.
> The feast shall cloy not, nor the chase shall tire,
> Nor music cease forever through the hall;
> The gold and jewels of the Land of Youth

Outshine all splendours ever dreamed by man.
Thou shalt have horses of the fairy breed,
Thou shalt have hounds that can outrun the wind;
A hundred chiefs shall follow thee in war,
A hundred maidens sing thee to thy sleep.
A crown of sovranty thy brow shall wear,
And by thy side a magic blade shall hang,
And thou shalt be lord of all the Land of Youth,
And lord of Niam of the Head of Gold.[5]

And as Niamh ended her song, so ended Oisín's time with the Fianna. Just as Oisín entered Fionn's life via a deer hunt and fairy woman, so he left it.

When the white horse with its riders reached the sea it ran lightly over the waves, and soon the green woods and headlands of Erin faded out of sight. And now the sun shone fiercely down, and the riders passed into a golden haze in which Oisin lost all knowledge of where he was or if sea or dry land were beneath his horse's hoofs. But strange sights sometimes appeared to them in the mist, for towers and palace gateways loomed up and disappeared, and once a horn-less doe bounded by them chased by a white hound with one red ear; and again they saw a young maid ride by on a brown steed, bearing a golden apple in her hand, and close behind her followed a young horseman on a white steed, a purple cloak floating at his back and a gold-hilted sword in his hand. And Oisin would have asked the princess who and what these apparitions were, but Niamh bade him ask nothing nor seem to notice any phantom they might see until they were come to the Land of Youth.[6]

Oisín spent three joyous years in Tír na nÓg and he and Niamh were married and had three children. Yet he longed to see Ireland and his comrades again and decided to return home. Unable to change his mind, Niamh gave him her white horse, Embarr, with the instructions not to set foot on the soil of Ireland or he would never be able to return to the Land of the Young. As Oisín passed over the mystic sea and once again set eyes on the rugged coastline of Ireland, an unpleasant surprise awaited him: the Ireland of the Fianna was gone. The hillforts with their great feasting halls were overgrown with ruins. In place of the tall, powerful heroes he was accustomed to were smaller, feeble people.

In some versions of the story, it's said that three centuries had passed and the age of heroes was over, and the age of St. Patrick had come. In other versions the passage of time is far longer. Fairy folklore is full of tales of missing time with moments spent in Fairyland being the equivalent of years, sometimes generations, on earth. There are many tales of those who return from their time with fairies to find their family and friends have long since died, or some telling of returners' bodies aging or decaying instantaneously the moment they touch other humans.

Oisín traversed Ireland looking for his comrades, and he came to a place called Glen of the Thrushes where he met some men struggling to move a great marble flagstone. They asked Oisín to help (in other versions of the story it is men in a quarry trying to move a large stone who need Oisín's help). Oisín moved the stone, but in the effort his horse's saddle girth broke and he fell to the ground. The moment he touched the soil of Ireland, Niamh's fears were realized and he aged several centuries instantly, transforming into a frail, blind old man.

In *Colloquy of the Ancients*, Oisín and his companion, Caílte mac Rónáin, remained alive until the time of Saint Patrick and told the saint the tales of the Fianna. In other renditions of the story, Caílte mac Rónáin is not present and, depending on whose version of the narrative you read, Oisín either defends the Fianna or accepts Christ as he recounts the story of his life to Patrick.

In *Gods and Fighting Men: The Story of the Tuatha de Danaan and of the Fiana of Ireland*, the dramatist and folklorist Lady Gregory sets out to reproduce Irish mythology in *Kiltartanese*—a term she coined for English with Gaelic syntax, based on the dialect spoken in Kiltartan,

County Galway. This was a conscious decision in order to convey the spirit of Irish mythology as well as its stories to the English-speaking world, a well-meaning attempt to replicate the original performance of these tales as they may have been told by the storytellers of Ireland.

Book XI, "Oisín and Patrick," is Lady Gregory's retelling of the discourse between the two iconic Irish figures. This chapter presents an interesting window into how the Irish mind had processed and reconciled the epistemological shift of the arrival of Christianity on the island. The story is symbolic of Christianity's accession over the native Irish beliefs, represented by Oisín. The poet Oisín held his own in the exchanges with Patrick; indeed one could argue that he illustrated the failings of Christian teaching on salvation when presented with the information that his companions and father were in hell.

> "It is God gained the victory over Finn," said Patrick, "and not the strong hand of an enemy; and as to the Fianna, they are condemned to hell along with him, and tormented forever."[7]

Faced with this injustice, Oisín gave an impassioned response to the patron saint, questioning how such a noble hero as Fionn could be in hell.

> "O Patrick, the story is pitiful, the King of the Fianna to be under locks; a heart without envy, without hatred, a heart hard in earning victory. It is an injustice, God to be unwilling to give food and riches; Finn never refused strong or poor, although cold Hell is now his dwelling-place."[8]

I imagine the people of Ireland may have shared Oisín's sentiment. Throughout the passage Oisín denigrates Patrick's monks and priests as "clerks" and reminds the saint continuously that were his former companions present, they would put him in his place and separate the heads of his clerks from their shoulders. The exchange betrays a tension in the Irish heart. The listeners long for the age of heroes. Who would not cheer on the fair-minded half-fairy hero against the rigid and proselytizing saint? This exchange represents a cultural dual practice that was outwardly Christian but also honored the old gods and beliefs.

Oisín's tale muddies the ontological waters, providing the Dark Man with a vehicle to exist in the slipstream of the Christian ideological behemoth as it overtook Ireland. Through the story and others, *he* exists in the imagination as an indeterminate fairy or devil. Of course, it would be remiss not to reference the Christian Devil as a significant vehicle of his survival. The primary distinction here is that the folklore in which the Dark Man lived was in the language of the people: Gaelic. The language of Christianity was Latin, which the population did not understand. Irish festivals and celebrations largely contained ancient pagan components alongside Christian ones, or the pagan hidden within the Christian messaging—an indication of the intertwined practices.

This dual practice is Irish culture's attempt to manage the forces that the Dark Man and fairies represent: chaos and nature within a Christian framework. An example of this dual practice can still be found in modern Ireland, in Killorglin, County Kerry, at the *Puck Fair*. The Puck Fair's main event is the capture of a wild billy goat that is then crowned King Puck. King Puck has a bride, traditionally a schoolgirl from one of the local primary schools. They are *married* and paraded around the town. This is the start of a three-day festival of music and drinking. Evidence suggests that the Fair existed long before written records were kept. The time of year strongly suggests that the event is linked to pre-Christian celebrations of Lughnasadh. The symbolic marriage is between the local community—represented by a girl on the cusp of womanhood—and the embodied wildness of the divine landscape in the form of the puck. A prepubescent girl marrying a wild goat, replete with impressive horns, is not subtle symbolism. The etymology of the word *puck* gives strong indication to what the goat represents—it is highly likely to be cognate to *Púca*. The Púca is a fairy creature considered to be a bringer of both good and bad fortune, best placated. The Púca can have dark or white fur or hair—a nondualistic motif in itself—and can shape-shift, taking the appearance of goats, cats, dogs, or hares. Púca could also assume human form but with animal features, just as the Dark Man may present. The Cornish equivalent is *Bucca*, to whom the contemporary witchcraft coven of Ros An Bucca pay homage in their rites. According to folklorist Máire MacNeill in her 1962 book, *The Festival of Lughnasa*, the primary narrative that emerges from the Lughnasadh folklore and rites is a conflict between two gods over the harvest. The grain is kept by one god, who is typically referred to as "Crom Dubh." In the conflict that ensues, Lugh and later St. Patrick wrest the grain from Crom Dubh to share among the people. Crom Dubh is likely the same figure as Crom Cruach and shares some qualities with the Daghdha and Donn,[9] further connections to the Dark One.

Dual practice is embodied by Oisín and perhaps this is the purpose behind the Dark Man's trickery. Oisín is a hybrid being: he is part human, part fairy; he belongs to both worlds and yet neither, existing outside human reality and yet in it. His very existence is a challenge to dualism. Oisín is not alone in this role; throughout mythology many significant figures have claimed similar ancestry. Staying within the British Isles, Merlin also represents an embodiment of dual belief. The magician is the child of the mortal woman and a succubus from whom he inherits his supernatural powers of prophecy, seership, and shape-shifting. Michael Dames, in his book *Merlin and Wales: A Magician's Landscape*, frames the purpose of Merlin and the motif of the wonder child as follows:

> To psychologists of the Jungian school, all these infants represent an archetype symbolizing "the pre-conscious aspect of the collective human psyche. If the child's gift is accepted, adult society may rediscover its 'original, unconscious and instinctive state.'[10]

This original primordial state is outside of, or perhaps more correctly, *before* duality. The wonder child is a mythological clue to the greater mysteries, bringing us back to the question posed at the start of this chapter. In the stories of Oisín's birth the Dark Man—acting as Fionn's adversary—sets these events in motion. Through his actions the fairy woman Sadhbh becomes Fionn's lover, and they conceive the hybrid child Oisín. The Dark Man then removes Sadhbh and later sends the boy back to his father, and Oisín's tale lasts a thousand years. It allows us to follow and recognize the current through the mythology in the Fear Dubh, Donn Dubh, the Daghdha, and beyond Irish mythology to Lucifer, the fallen angel light bringer.

4
The Dark Interceptor

Don't come around tonight
Well, it's bound to take your life
There's a bad moon on the rise

"Bad Moon Rising"
by Creedence Clearwater Revival

The roads we travel are liminal in nature. They are in-between places that connect everything and everywhere. The road exposes vulnerability and promises adventure. Even with modern convenience, we're no strangers to the challenges travel can present: the threat of crime, the plans gone awry. Traveling is full of uncertainty, and it forces the traveler to adapt as the road dictates the way and one has little choice but to navigate as best one can. To travel is to leave the safety of our homes . . . and sometimes the safety of the human world. Otherworldly dangers can intercept the traveler when they are at their most vulnerable.

In Devon, England, in the 1920s, there was a phenomenon known as the Hairy Hands. Witnesses reported a pair of hairy phantom hands wrenching control of their vehicle from them and driving them off the road, causing many accidents along the road known as the B3212. The story eventually caught the attention of the UK media. The BBC's account of the story reported:

It seems though that it's not just motorists that are at risk from the devil's digits, any campers in the area have need to fear too. In

42

1924 a young couple were camping in a caravan in the area and the woman was woken in the middle of the night by a heart-racing fear. Her bunk faced the caravan window and up it she saw crawling a large hand, covered in hair and, she said, exuding an intent to do her and her husband harm. Instinctively the lady made the sign of the cross and said the hand balked and made its way away.[1]

These strange events led to the road being reworked. But what of the witnesses? How did they change? Was their worldview challenged? Their confidence in the nature of reality shaken? Here we may see the pattern of the Dark Man at work.

We can't describe the dangers of the road without discussing the crossroads. Orion Foxwood explained to me that in his tradition, the Dark Man is also known as the Dark Rider and the Lord of the Crossroads. In America, the first crossroads followed animal migration, which in turn followed the magnetic ley lines of the earth, and where one crossed the other a well of power forms. These are the places that are most potent for calling the Dark Rider.

Magister, Coven of Heth Pontifex, Robin Artisson writes:

When you stand at the crossroads, you are standing in the realization that you have a serious choice to make. On the left hand, there is a grinding storm of pain and terror, of blind, drunk passions and wonderful imagination and ideas. That is the way of death, though if you were to go that way, you would find yourself very much alive. On the other hand, the right hand, there is a great, mysterious freedom, something you cannot even begin to gaze upon, and which offers no clean assurances. That is the way of life, though if you were to go that way it might mean the death of everything you've known, cherished and loved.[2]

Whether you have sought out the Dark Man or he has intercepted you, significant change will surely be coming. The nature of that change depends on how you react. The folklore of Britain and Ireland are full of tales of supernatural interceptors that lie in wait for travelers under bridges and on lonely roads. A search for the terms *Dark Man* or *Fear Dubh* on the Irish National Folklore Collection website, Dúchas .ie, will return dozens of such accounts. The stories have similar structure. A person is traveling when they are intercepted by a large man in black—often on a horse—who terrifies them in some way. In one story the Dark Man demonstrates his infernal powers by producing a ball of fire from his coat, at which the traveler turns tail and runs (no doubt a wise decision). In other versions the Dark Man has cloven hooves or a large black dog. He may appear in the passenger seat of a farmer's cart, never once responding to attempts at conversation, before disappearing and leaving the farmer petrified. These tales may also be used to explain features of the landscape:

> One evening a maid was going with the tea to some workmen in a field near Tobermannan bridge when she saw a dark man standing on the bridge. At sight of her he began to walk quickly. He had just gone three steps when fire blazed forth from his mouth. At that moment the basket fell from the maid's hand and the griddle cake fell out on the bank of the river where it immediately disappeared. There is a large stone shaped like a griddle-cake to be seen in the spot where the griddle cake fell.[3]

Here the mysterious presence provides an explanation of a quirk of the landscape. The dark man is a terrifying and transmutative force, turning the griddle cake into stone. He demonstrates mastery over the material world along with an agenda that is beyond human understanding.

I term this aspect of the Dark Man "The Dark Interceptor." The details in these accounts fluctuate but there is a recognizable pattern. The Dark Man's horse can be black or white, and sometimes the horse has eyes like red hot coals. The rider tends to be dressed in the finery of a nobleman and is, as the name suggests, head to toe in black. The following tale, "The Dark Horseman,"[4] is from *Ancient Legends of Ireland* by Lady Wilde.

One day a fine, handsome young fellow, called Jemmy Nowlan, set off to walk to the fair at Slane, whither some cattle of his had been sent off for sale that same morning early. And he was dressed in his best clothes, spruce and neat; and not one in all the county round could equal Jemmy Nowlan for height, strength, or good looks. So he went along quite gay and merry in himself, till he came to a lonely bit of the road where never a soul was to be seen; but just then the sky became black-dark, as if thunder were in the air, and suddenly he heard the tramp of a horse behind him. On turning round he saw a very dark, elegant looking gentleman, mounted on a black horse, riding swiftly towards him. "Jemmy Nowlan," said the dark horse-man, "I have been looking for you all along the road. Get up now, quickly, behind me, and I'll carry you in no time to the great fair of Slane; for, indeed, I am going there myself, and it would be very pleasant to have your company. "Thank your honour kindly," said Jemmy; "but it's not for the likes of me to ride with your lordship; so I would rather walk, if it's pleasing to your honour; but thanks all the same."

Truth to tell, Jemmy in his own mind had a fear of the strange gentleman and his black horse, and distrusted them both, for had he not heard the people tell strange stories of how young men had been carried off by the fairies, and held prisoners by their enchantments down deep in the heart of the hill under the earth, where never a mortal could see them again or know their fate; and they were only allowed to come up and see their kindred on the nights the dead walked, and then they walked with them as they rose from the graves? So again he began to make his excuses, and meanwhile kept looking round for some path by which he could escape if possible.

"Come now," said the dark horseman, "this is all nonsense, Jemmy Nowlan; you really must come with me."

And with that he stooped down and touched him lightly on the shoulder with his whip, and in an instant Jemmy found himself seated on the horse, and galloping away like the wind with the dark horseman; and they never stopped nor stayed till they came to a great castle in a wood, where a whole set of servants in green and gold were waiting on the steps to receive them. And they were the smallest people Jemmy had ever seen in his life; but he made no remark, for they were very civil, and crowded round to know what they could do for him.

"Take him to a room and let him dress," said the gentleman, who appeared to own the castle. And in the room Jemmy found a beautiful suit of velvet, and a cap and feather. And when the little servants had dressed him they led him to the large hall that was all lit up and hung with garlands of flowers; and music and dancing were going on, and many lovely ladies were present, but not one in the hall was handsomer than Jemmy Nowlan in his velvet suit and cap and feather. "Will you dance with me, Jemmy Nowlan?" said one lovely lady. "No, Jemmy: you must dance with me," said another. And they all fought for him, so he danced with them all, one after the other, the whole night through, till he was dead tired and longed to lie down and sleep.

"Take Jemmy Nowlan to his room, and put him to bed," said the gentleman to a red-haired man; "but first he must tell me a story."

"I have no story, your honour," said Jemmy, "for I am not book-learned; but I am very tired, let me lie down and sleep." "Sleep, indeed," said the gentleman; "not if I can help it. Here, Davy"—and he called the red-haired man—"take Jemmy Nowlan and put him out; he can tell no story. I will have no one here who can't tell me a story. Put him out, he is not worth his supper."

So the red-haired man thrust Jemmy out at the castle gate, and he was just settling himself to sleep on a bench outside, when three men came by bearing a coffin.

"Oho, Jemmy Nowlan," they said, "you are welcome. We just wanted a fourth man to carry the coffin."

And they made him get under it with them, and away they marched over hedge and ditch, and field and bog, through briars and thorns, till they reached the old churchyard in the valley, and then they stopped.

"Who will dig a grave?" said one. "Let us draw lots," said another. And the lot fell on Jemmy. So they gave him a spade, and he worked till the grave was dug broad and deep.

"This is not the right place at all for a grave," said the leader of the party when the grave was finished. "I'll have no one buried in this spot, for the bones of my father rest here." So they had to take up the coffin again, and carry it on over field and bog till they reached another churchyard, where Jemmy was obliged to dig a second grave; and when it was finished, the leader cried out

"Who shall we place in the coffin?" And another voice answered, "We need draw no lots; lay Jemmy Nowlan in the coffin!"

And the men seized hold of him and tried to cast him to the ground. But Jemmy was strong and powerful, and fought them all. Still they would not let go their hold, though he dealt them such blows as would have killed any other men. At last he felt faint, for he had no weapon to fight with, and his strength was going.

Then he saw that the leader carried a hazel switch in his hand, and he knew that a hazel switch brought luck; so he made a sudden spring and seized it, and whirled it three times round his head, and struck right and left at his assailants, when a strange and wondrous thing happened; for the three men who were ready to kill him, fell down at once to the ground, and remained there still as the dead. And the coffin stood white in the moonlight by itself, and no hand touched it, and no voice spoke.

But Jemmy never waited to look or think, for the fear of the men was on him, lest they should rise up again; so he fled away, still holding the hazel twig in his hand, and ran on over field and bog, through briars and thorns, till he found himself again at the castle gate. Then all the grand servants came out, and the little men, and they said "You are welcome, Jemmy Nowlan. Come in; his lordship is waiting for you."

And they brought him to a room where the lord was lying on a velvet couch, and he said "Now, young man, tell me a story, for no one in my castle is allowed to eat, drink, or sleep till they have related something wonderful that has happened to them."

"Then, my lord," said Jemmy, "I can tell you the most wonderful of stories; and very proud I am to be able to amuse your lordship."

So he told him the story of the three men and the coffin, and the lord was so pleased that he ordered the servants to bring the youth a fine supper, and the best of wine, and Jemmy ate like a prince from gold dishes, and drank from crystal cups of the wine, and had the best of everything; but after the supper he felt rather queer and dazed-like, and fell down on the ground asleep like one dead. After that he knew nothing till he awoke next morning, and found himself lying under a haystack in his own field, and all his beautiful clothes were gone—the velvet suit and cap and feather that he had looked so handsome in at the dance, when all the fine ladies fell in love with him. Nothing was left to him of all the night's adventure save the hazel twig, which he still held firmly in his hand.

And a very sad and down-hearted man was Jemmy Nowlan that day, especially when the herd came to tell him that none of the cattle were sold at the fair, for the men were waiting for the master, and wondering why he did not come to look after his money, while all the other farmers were selling their stock at the finest prices.

And Jemmy Nowlan has never yet made out why the fairies played him such a malicious and ill turn as to prevent him selling his cattle. But if ever again he meets that dark stranger on the black horse, he is determined to try the strength of his shillelagh on his head, were he ever such a grand man among the fairies. For at least he might have left him the velvet suit; and it was a shabby thing to take it away just when he couldn't help himself, and had fallen down from fair weakness and exhaustion after all the dancing, and the wine he drank at supper, when the lovely ladies poured it out for him with their little hands covered with jewels.

It was truly a bad and shabby trick, as Jemmy said to himself that May morning, when he stood up from under the hay-rick; and just shows us never to trust the fairies, for with all their sweet words and pleasant ways and bright red wine, they are full of malice and envy and deceit, and are always ready to ruin a poor fellow and then laugh at him, just for fun, and for the spite and jealousy they have against the human race.

In deconstructing the story we note Jemmy is described as a hand-some young man. Spirited away to the dark horseman's palace, Jemmy concerns himself with looking well and entertaining the fairer sex. When pushed by the dark horseman, he has nothing to say, no story to tell, and he loses favor: without a story to tell, he finds himself cast aside and fight-ing for his life with adversaries that would put him in his grave. Note that he uses a hazel wand to break their hold on him and he returns to the dark horseman and tells his tale and is rewarded. When Jemmy wakes up, his finery is gone and none of his cattle are sold at the market.

Having "no story to tell" is analogous to having no depth. Jemmy is forced to face his own death and is left with little the morning after. He learns that death can come at any moment, and nothing is more fleeting than youth and beauty. Most of all he learns to be wary of the fairies. It is a shabby trick, which questions his worldview and values.

We stay with Lady Wilde for another interrupted journey, "The Ride with the Fairies."[5]

Once on a time a gentleman, also one of the Kirwans of Galway, was riding by the fairy hill—where all the fairies of the West hold their councils and meetings, under the rule of Finvarra the king—when a strange horseman, mounted on a fiery black steed, sud-denly appeared. But as the stranger bid him the time of day with distinguished grace, Mr. Kirwan returned his greeting courteously, and they rode on together side by side, discoursing pleasantly for the stranger seemed to know everyone and everything, though Mr. Kirwan could not remember ever having seen him before.

"Now," said the black horseman, "I know that you are to be at the races to-morrow, so just let me give you a hint: if you wish to be certain of winning, allow me to send you my man to ride your horse. He never failed in a race yet, and he shall be with you early, before the start." With that, at a turn of the road, the stranger disappeared; for he was no other than Finvarra himself, who had a friendly liking for the tribe of the Kirwans, because all the men were generous who came of the blood, and all the women handsome. Next morning, as Mr. Kirwan was setting out for the race, his groom told him that a young jockey was waiting to see him. He was the strangest looking little imp, Mr. Kirwan thought, he had ever set eyes on, but he felt compelled to give him all the rights and power that was necessary for the race, and the young imp was off in a moment, like a flash of lightning.

In this story the Dark Man, Finvarra, is a composite figure of the Fairy King, Devil, and Lord of the Dead. He has a fondness for the Kirwan family as they are generous and handsome, and he watches over their bloodline.

Mr. Kirwan knew no more—he seemed like one in a dream till the silver cup was handed to him as winner of the race, and congratulations poured down on him, and every one asked eagerly where he got the wonderful jockey who seemed to make the horse fly like the spirit of the wind itself. But the jockey by this time had disappeared. However, the stranger on the black horse was there, and he constrained Mr. Kirwan to come with him to dinner; and they rode on pleasantly, as before, till they reached a grand, beautiful house, with a crowd of gorgeous servants waiting on the steps to receive the lord and master and his guest.

One of them led Mr. Kirwan to his room to dress for dinner, and there he found a costly suit of violet velvet ready, in which the valet arrayed him. Then he entered the dining-hall. It was all lit up splendidly, and there were garlands of flowers twining round crystal columns, and golden cups set with jewels for the wine, and golden dishes. The host seemed an accomplished man of the world, and did the honours with perfect grace. Conversation flowed freely, while soft music was heard at intervals from invisible players, and Mr. Kirwan could not resist the charm and beauty of the scene, nor the bright red wine that his host poured out for him into the jewelled cups.

Then, when the banquet was over, a great crowd of ladies and gentlemen came in and danced to sweet low music, and they circled round the guest and tried to draw him into the dance. But when he looked at them it seemed to him that they were all the dead he had once known; for his own brother was there, that had been drowned in the lake a year before; and a man who had been killed by a fall when hunting; and others whose faces he knew well. And they were all pale as death, but their eyes burned like coals of fire.

And as he looked and wondered, a lovely lady came over to him, wearing a necklace of pearls. And she clasped his wrist with her little hand, and tried to draw him into the circle. "Dance with me," she whispered, "dance with me again. Look at me, for you once loved me." And when he looked at her he knew that she was dead, and the clasp of her hand was like a ring of fire round his wrist; and he drew back in terror, for he saw that she was a beautiful girl he had loved in his youth, and to whom he had given a necklace of pearls, but who died before he could make her his bride.

Then his heart sank with fear and dread, and he said to his host "Take me from this place. I know the dancers; they are dead. Why have you brought them up from their graves?"

But the host only laughed and said, "You must take more wine to keep up your courage." And he poured him out a goblet of wine redder than rubies.

And when he drank it, all the pageant and the music and the crowd faded away from before his eyes, and he fell into a profound sleep, and knew no more till he found himself at home, laid on his bed. And the servant told him that a strange horse man had accompanied him to the door late in the night, who had charged them to lay the master gently in his bed and by no means to awake him till noon next day, for he was weary after the race; and he bade them take the hunter to the stables and tend him carefully, for the animal was covered with foam, and all trembling.

At noon Mr. Kirwan awoke, and rose up as well as ever: but of all the fairy revels nothing remained to him but the mark round his wrist of the clasp of a woman's hand, that seemed burned into his flesh So he knew the night's adventure was no mere dream of the fancy, and the mark of the dead hand remained with him to his last hour, and the form of the young girl with her necklace of pearls often came before him in a vision of the night; but he never again visited the fairy palace, and never saw the dark horseman any more. As to the silver cup, he flung it into the lake, for he thought it had come to him by devil's magic and would bring no good luck to him or to his race. So it sank beneath the waves, and the silver cup was seen no more.

Here we have the themes of abduction, death, and the passing of youth and beauty once more. Mr. Kirwan is taken to a palace in a fairy land of the dead where he undergoes his ordeal. He is presented with symbols of material wealth: a velvet suit, a crystal pillared palace, gold cups and dishes. He is then confronted with friends and loved ones he has lost to death. In his moment of despair, he is instructed to drink more and have courage. He does so, faces his fear, and survives. He remains scared and haunted by the experience and casts away the silver cup because his values have changed, and his understanding of the world has been upturned.

Once the Dark Man appears chaos follows, and in his wake

there is true illumination. He offers a choice: change or collapse, persevere or suffer. In both of these stories, the illusions of material reality are shattered; material wealth loses its value; the opulent feast becomes an ordeal. Kirwan experiences death and revulsion contrasted with life and desire, embodied by his dead lover. This is a metaphor on the limitations of dualism. The Dark Man encounter can dissolve one's egoic illusion, or *Maya*. Maya is a fundamental concept within the nondualist Advaita, an influential school within Vedanta, and one of the six orthodox philosophical systems of Indian philosophy.

> Maya is reflected on the individual level by human ignorance (ajnana) of the real nature of the self, which is mistaken for the empirical ego but which is in reality identical with brahman.[6]

While these stories focused on the physically intercepted journey, in actuality it is the *life journey* where the interception happens. With the Dark Man there are always layers of meaning. We never get to the center of these layers because it is not possible for us to do so. The Dark Man shocks us to remind us to follow our soul's purpose. Often that purpose is one that serves his agenda. Irish storyteller Eddie Lenihan speaks of the fairies needing humans for their business, whatever that business might be. The same applies to the Dark Man, and what that business might be only the Devil knows.

The Interceptor is not confined to the lonely country roads of rural Britain and Ireland; he is all around us today. Through the storytellers he maintains his presence in our cultural language. Think of the dark men in contemporary media, from *The Hitcher* to *Fargo*'s Lorne Malvo, to every spaghetti western's man-with-no-name: they are characters cut from the same cloth as the Dark Interceptor. He lives in our stories and shows us just enough that we might recognize him if our paths cross. Should you meet him, some will turn tail and run. There's no shame in it either. It's probably the most prudent thing to do.

Because some roads you shouldn't go down. Because maps used to say, "There be dragons here." Now they don't. But that don't mean the dragons aren't there.

LORNE MALVO, FARGO

Yet some of us are compelled to go down Malvo's roads. Perhaps part of us needs to meet what's waiting there despite our fears. Maybe there's a would-be fire in our blood that needs a dragon to ignite it.

5

Tricky Trickster, Culture Changer

Just like the pied piper
Led rats through the streets
We dance like marionettes
Swaying to the symphony of destruction
"SYMPHONY OF DESTRUCTION" BY MEGADETH

The trickster is a vector of chaos and change. He shakes up our lives and understandings with all manner of wicked tricks, wonders, terrors, and deliberate contradictions. He laughs at our plans and ambitions, sending us down blind alleys and on fool's errands. He exasperates with nonsensical communication peppered with revelations. He leads us in circles and defies categorization. Ultimately he calls us to initiation. If we pay close attention, we might just get the joke. If we listen without discernment, we might be the punchline.

There is an instinct in many of us to break the rules and push the boundaries, often without really knowing why. The trickster is the cutting edge of chaos. He punctures convention to unsettle reality with novelty. When the forces of order begin to stagnate, the trickster may arrive to create enough disorder to rebalance the world. Once the dust has settled, we find ourselves in a new landscape where the mountains of convention and consensus have crumbled into the sea. But when the trickster goes too far, as he frequently does, a hero representing the forces of order rides in to reestablish balance. It is a story as old as time—just ask Adam and Eve.

If we look back over the folklore discussed in earlier chapters, we see trickery in the behavior of the Dark Man and his adjacent characters. Donn Dubh lures the Fianna into his palace by turning a fairy woman into a deer for them to hunt. The Dark Rider offers Mr. Kirwan his help in a race that takes him on a horrifying confrontation with the dead in the otherworld. The trickster warns us not to accept the status quo. One could argue that the horror of an encounter with the Dark Man is a trick in itself. The dark silhouette that invades our dreams is the trick that becomes impossible to ignore. The same can be said of the paranormal phenomena that defy rationality and yet persist regardless. As Patrick Harpur brilliantly surmises:

> All daimons are tricksters, as the fairies are; all are in the pay of Hermes-Mercurius. He unsettles our lives with all manner of impish tricks and pixilations; the more we ignore him, the more he bedevils us, until his tricks begin to look sinister. He becomes, in fact, the Devil.[1]

I think Harpur's framing is circling the truth here. The trickster current, like the creative current, flows through these strange entities. While they are not necessarily emanations of the Dark One, they seem to be subject to his will and eager to serve him. The Gods are not immune from the trickster's hoaxes either: from Anansi and the Sky God Nyame to Hermes and Apollo, the trickster shakes the snow globe of order ensuring novelty for all. There is an array of tools in his bag to instigate change: accidents, paranormal anomalies . . . the trickster spins the wheel of fortune, putting a question mark on both our consensus and individual realities.

In my first chapter I discussed the devil footprints seen in Devon, England, and the wooden carving of the horned devil overlooking St. Mary's church in Swansea, Wales. Forteana of this nature has always been attributed to the Dark One. Europe during the Middle Ages was a rich hunting ground for our prank-happy trickster friend, and thirteenth-century Germany was the backdrop for one of the most famous abduction stories of all time: that of the Pied Piper of Hamelin. Bernard Queenan writes in "Evolution of the Pied Piper" that the earliest surviving written version originated around 1370, as an endnote in a copy of Heinrich von Herod's *Catena Aurea*,[2] originally written in Latin:

> To be noted is a marvellous and truly extraordinary event that occurred in the town of Hamelin in the diocese of Minden in the year of the Lord 1284, on the very feast-day of Saints John and Paul. A young man of 30 years, handsome and in all respects so finely dressed that all who saw him were awestruck by his person and clothing came in by way of the bridge and the Weser Gate. On a silver pipe which he had, of wonderful form, he began to play through the whole town, and all the children hearing him, to the number of 130, followed him beyond the eastern wall almost to the place of the Calvary or Gallows field, and vanished and disappeared so that nobody could find out where any one of them had gone. Indeed, the mothers of the children wandered from city to city and discovered nothing. A voice was heard in Rama and every mother bewailed her son. And as people count by the years of the Lord or by the first, second and third after a jubilee, so they have counted in Hamelin by the first, second and third year after the exodus and departure of the children. This I have found in an old book. And the mother of Herr Johann de Lude, the deacon, saw the children going out.[3]

The Pied Piper had relieved the town of its rat infestation, as per his agreement with the mayor, by drowning the rodents in the nearby Weser River. The mayor then reneged on the deal, sending the Pied Piper packing with a paltry sum and the rest is history . . . well, folkloric history. A number of interesting themes stand out. The Piper is a stranger who arrives at the peak of the town's despair. In certain versions of the story, he's described as handsome, and is notably in possession of a silver flute. The silver denotes its rarity and, by extension, its enchantment. Pipers are consistently associated with fairies across Europe, and those of exceptional talent in Ireland often claimed to have learned their skill while in Fairyland or would attribute the inspiration for a particular air to having fallen asleep on a fairy fort. *Pied* is a reference to his multicolored attire, and he's frequently depicted in bright stripes or diamond patterns associated with a jester. By enchanting the rats, he demonstrates a mastery over animals, which is a typical trope of shamans the world over. In the Piper's case, he also charms Hamelin's

Fig. 4. The oldest picture of the Pied Piper copied from
the glass window of the Market Church in Hamelin, Germany (c.1300–1633).
Note the cave entrance to the otherworld in the top right.
Wikimedia Commons

children. Some versions describe how the children dance uncontrollably to a nearby cave in a hill where a door opens, and the Piper leads them through to Fairyland. In other versions of the story, a child who is lame and cannot keep up with the dancing children witnesses them all passing into Fairyland before the door slams shut. The mayor and the townspeople are punished for their avarice in a staggeringly cruel way, and this serves as a reminder that it is unwise to breach a contract, especially one made with the Devil. The punishment was so severe that we're still talking about it 750 years later.

As far-fetched as it seems, the story has some historical basis. There were numerous cases of dancing mania, or choreomania, throughout the Middle Ages involving groups of children and adults dancing manically to the point of collapse. This was known as "the dancing plague." Accounts describe people dancing for days, even months, like marionettes on a string. Who or what was the puppeteer? One theory was Ergotism, or ergot poisoning from a mold that grew on stalks of ripening rye. When eaten this can cause hallucinations, spasms, and tremors. John Waller argued against this theory in *The Lancet*:

> This theory does not seem tenable, since it is unlikely that those poisoned by ergot could have danced for days at a time. Nor would so many people have reacted to its psychotropic chemicals in the same way. The ergotism theory also fails to explain why virtually every outbreak occurred somewhere along the Rhine and Moselle Rivers, areas linked by water but with quite different climates and crops.[4]

Returning to Victorian England, we find Spring-heeled Jack, a devilish anomaly with the outlandish ability to leap great heights. Spring-heeled Jack first appeared in the 1800s, terrifying the people of London and farther afield, and being reported in local press and in accounts of the time. In October 1837 a young woman by the name of

Mary Stevens was accosted while walking through London's Clapham Common. Her clothes were ripped and she was touched by her attacker's claws, which she reported as being, "cold and clammy as those of a corpse."[5] Thankfully Mary's screams were enough to drive off her attacker, and he disappeared into the London night. The following day came the report of another incident around the same area of London, in which a similar figure had jumped in front of a carriage, causing it to crash. Witnesses reported him leaping over a nine-foot wall and escaping while cackling with high-pitched laughter.[6] Spring-heeled Jack—as he came to be known in the press—was described as having eyes like burning red fire, clawed hands, a helmet, and white oilskin clothing beneath a black cloak. Others describe a bearlike appearance, or one like a ghost.

Of each of Spring-heeled Jack's appearances, the 1838 assault on eighteen-year-old Jane Alsop was the most sensationalized. Her description resembled that given by Mary Stevens, including the phantom's appearance, but with an additional detail: the being spat blue and white fire into her face. Two days earlier, in London's docklands area, Lucy Scales and her sister were also accosted by a stranger who spat blue fire in their faces.[7] He was cloaked and tall and thin—this last detail brings to mind the story of the Dark Man and the griddle cake stone on Tobermannan bridge. After dozens of sightings across London and across the UK, Spring-heeled Jack became a byword for the boogey man, representing the dangers of the unknown and inexplicable. The attacks took place at the peak of the British Empire, as "civility and rationality" was a justification for British Imperialism on Indigenous peoples. Under this guise, British Imperialism and its ideological predecessors had been perfected on the Celtic peoples of Britain and Ireland before being exported throughout the world. Meanwhile the citizens of the empire's capital watched the rooftops in fear of a fire-breathing devil. As if to underline the point, the last cluster of sightings was in 1877 at the Aldershot Garrison in Southeast England. Aldershot was known as the home of the British Army, which was then the most powerful military force in the world with roughly ten thousand troops. And yet this robustly secure site was chosen by Jack to strike in a series of attacks:

> On several occasions he appeared at lonely sentry boxes in outlying parts of the camp, clambering onto sentry boxes and passing an ice-cold hand over the faces of the startled soldiers within, then making off across the heath with his usual agility. At least twice the sentries recovered their composure in time to loose a round in his direction, but if any of the balls struck home, the phantom attacker showed no sign he had been hurt. And in the autumn he returned, repeating his antics of the spring.[8]

Jack was untouchable, repeatedly and obtusely striking at the heart of the British military with impunity. What message would the British public take from these events? An empire that ruled over a fifth of the earth was confounded by a cackling devil with an ice-cold touch, appearing and disappearing at will to wreak havoc. Was this enough to undermine faith in the authority of the empire and the rule of law? Of course not. But in the hearts of the victims, the witnesses, and those who heard the tale, the world had been turned upside-down. An ontological apocalypse left them nodes of enchantment, who would tell their stories or have stories told about them.

The industrial revolution began in Britain and transformed the country by the mid-nineteenth century. The population more than doubled within fifty years (from 8.3 million to 16.8 million). This population boom went hand in hand with urbanization, and modernity was the driving force of order, which enforced, and was supported by, a rigid class structure. As populations moved from rural landscapes and proximity to wildness to the factories and city slums, Jack reminded the populace that there was still a supernatural reason to fear the dark. He brought the fears of the wildlands to the cities, reminding the populace that while they may have forgotten the devil, the devil had not forgotten them.

Spring-heeled Jack faded from British consciousness as the century closed and would soon be remembered as a Victorian fantasy from the pages of some penny dreadful rather than for the real terror he represented. Every generation assumes it is superior in intellect to the ones that came before, and historical anomalies like Spring-heeled Jack are often dismissed as the product of the wild imagination of an uneducated and superstitious people. However, in 2012 the *Sutton & Croydon Guardian*—an English regional newspaper—reported the following:

> Scott Martin and his family were travelling home by taxi on Tuesday, February 14, at about 10.30pm when they saw the terrifying figure they have likened to the legendary Spring Heeled Jack dart across the road before leaping 15ft over a bank as they approached Nescot College on the Ewell bypass.[9]

The family described the being as a "dark figure with no features." The article goes on to recount a similar event from a few years earlier in which a terrified woman crashed her car to avoid a dark figure crossing the road. These accounts remind us that we are no more immune to the devilish trickster than our ancestors.

In 2013 a similar account of a dark figure was shared on the website Your Ghost Stories by a site member from County Offaly, Ireland. A friend of the poster's uncle found himself driving down a road in Ballycumber when he saw a completely black figure, roughly seven to eight feet in height, standing on the road. Terrified, he attempted to reverse, but when he looked over his shoulder and then back, the figure had mysteriously appeared right in front of his car and placed its hands, which were white (note the nondualism), on the car's bonnet, prompting him to hastily exit the car and run. Glancing back, the figure had vanished.

In another incident, a neighbor of the original poster's aunt phoned to report a black figure standing outside her house, peering into the sitting room window.

While walking his dog in a forest, the author's godfather and a friend encountered a black figure blocking their path. Terrified, they attempted to escape when their dog broke free and ran straight through the black figure.

On a separate night, the aunt awoke to find a black figure's face beside her. The figure stood, walked to the window, and gazed out before disappearing.[10]

This report concisely covers the principal patterns of the Dark Man. The apparition makes an interception on the road and performs impossible feats. He turns from black to partially white, suggesting light coming from the darkness. He is terrifying but helps someone in distress. The figure has an ambiguous interest in the family and draws people together through his presence. He is seen watching them: it is common for those with psychic abilities to see the Dark Man in some form around those he follows (as will be outlined in section two of this book). The apparition is seen among trees, in nature, blocking the way, and demanding attention, so much so that the witnesses run through a lake to escape. Attempts to rationalize what happened would be futile. Temporary comfort could be gained, but the Dark One would return, perhaps until he was recognized as real.

The individual here was driven to share these experiences online in search of answers to the troubling events. Upheaval of one's understanding of reality occurs with the arrival of the Dark Man. The foundations on which a worldview is built become unsound and may need to be abandoned, making space for a new structure, one that accommodates the anomalous and the paranormal despite the limitations of human understanding and the restrictions of scientism. The trickster's function is realized.

The trickster can achieve similar results on a societal level through driving culture change. In a multigenerational game, the culture changer sets events in motion through strange and confusing interjections.

In Cairo in 1904, the honeymoon of a young British couple took a turn when an entranced Rose Edith Crowley instructed her new husband, Aleister Crowley, that he must sit at his desk at noon April 8th and write down what he heard. He complied as instructed, and at precisely noon a voice began to dictate what would become known as "Liber Al Vel Legis" or "The Book of the Law," the central text of the magical current of Thelema. In his 1936 book, *The Equinox of the Gods*, Aleister Crowley gave an in-depth account of his encounter with the voice, stating "The Voice of Aiwass came apparently from over my left shoulder, from the furthest corner of the room."[11] If one interprets this experience from a folkloric perspective, the voice coming over the left shoulder is an interesting detail, as left—or *sinstra*—is associated with evil or chaos. While a simplistic analogy, the metaphor of the devil on the shoulder whispering mischief in one's ear has context here. This is the root of the superstition of throwing salt over the left shoulder. Spilling valuable salt is supposed to bring bad luck, and throwing the salt over your left shoulder blinds the devil so he doesn't know on whom to place the bad luck. In Crowley's account the voice comes from the corner of the room, a point of intersection and a common site of spirit entry.

> I had a strong impression that the speaker was actually in the corner where he seemed to be, in a body of "fine matter," transparent as a veil of gauze, or a cloud of incense-smoke. He seemed to be a tall, dark man in his thirties, well-knit, active and strong, with the face of a savage king, and eyes veiled lest their gaze should destroy what they saw. The dress was not Arab; it suggested Assyria or Persia, but very vaguely. I took little note of it, for to me at that time Aiwass was an "angel" such as I had often seen in visions, a being purely astral.[12]

Reading the description of Aiwass appearing as smoke, dressed in oriental garb, and having a kingly presence, one could be forgiven for thinking that Crowley encountered a djinn king, which would be entirely fitting given the setting. Certainly the local residents of Cairo would view the apparition as such. Crowley goes on to describe Aiwass as his personal holy guardian angel, a daimon he believed to be an "objective individual" and not an "abstraction" of himself.

> I now incline to believe that Aiwass is not only the God once held holy in Sumer, and mine own Guardian Angel, but also a man as I am, insofar as He uses a human body to make His magical link with Mankind, whom He loves, and that He is thus an Ipsissimus, the Head of the A∴A∴.[13]

In *Magick in Theory and Practice*, Crowley is resolute in identifying Aiwass as "the Devil," "Lucifer," and "Satan," whose emblem is the hermaphroditic goat Baphomet.[14] While this tale is remarkable in its own right, the purpose of the chapter is to examine the trickster as a cultural force and an agent of change. Crowley had a substantial impact on the arts: examples include his appearance on the cover of the Beatles' 1967 *Sgt. Pepper's Lonely Hearts Club Band* album and Jimmy Page buying his former home—The Boleskine House—at Loch Ness. And, in my view, it's possible to trace a thread of influence from the Aiwass initial contact to space flight via Crowley's follower, magician and rocket scientist Jack Parsons.

Parsons was a founding member of JPL (Jet Propulsion Laboratory, which was transferred to NASA in 1958). Much has been written about his Babalon Working: a series of magical workings or practices aimed at manifesting an incarnation of the archetypal divine feminine, Babalon, but it is Parsons's recognition as one of the most important figures in the history of space flight that is significant. His occult beliefs played a key part in his scientific ambitions, and he would passionately recite Crowley's "Hymn to Pan" during rocket tests. The invention and subsequent development of rocket technology changed humanity's fortunes forever.

The culture changer's presence is found elsewhere in the technological advances of the twentieth century. In a 1965 U.S. television broadcast, the "Father of the Atomic Bomb" J. Robert Oppenheimer reflected on witnessing the first successful atomic bomb test in Trinity, New Mexico:

> We knew the world would not be the same. A few people laughed, a few people cried. Most people were silent. I remembered the line from the Hindu scripture, the Bhagavad-Gita; Vishnu is trying to persuade the Prince that he should do his duty, and to impress him, takes on his multi-armed form and says, "Now I am become Death, the destroyer of worlds." I suppose we all thought that, one way or another.[15]

The exchange Oppenheimer is referring to is between Prince Arjuna and his charioteer Lord Krishna (an avatar of Vishnu and the supreme god in his own right). Arjuna's resolve falters at the battle of Kurukshetra when he is faced with the slaughter to come. Krishna reassures the prince, revealing to him the meaning of his dharma, his duty as a warrior, and the information that his enemies are already destroyed irrespective of Arjuna's choices. *Krishna* can mean "black," "swarthy," or "blue," and hence he is often depicted with blue skin. He is the archetypal mischievous trickster. As a libidinous boy-god, he seduces the village girls and steals curds and butter. He teases and dances with the Gopi milk maids, driving them mad with love. The poetess Mirabai, a devotee of Krishna, describes his effect in the poem "O I Saw Witchcraft Tonight."[16]

> *O I saw witchcraft tonight*
> *in the region of Braj.*
> *A milking girl going her rounds,*
> *a pot on her head,*
> *came face to face with the Dark One.*

My friend, she is babbling,
can no longer say "buttermilk."
—Come get the Dark One, the Dark One!
A pot full of Shyam!—
In the overgrown lanes
of Vrindavan forest
the Enchanter of Hearts fixed his
eye on this girl,
then departed.
Mira's lord is hot, lovely
and raven—
tonight she saw witchcraft
at Braj.

Another story of Krishna as a child involves his mother, Yashoda. When told that her son has been seen eating dirt, she reprimands him, demanding to know why he has done so. Krishna denies the charge and Yashoda asks him to open his mouth to prove it. Krishna does so and inside his mouth Yashoda sees the stars, the planets, and the entire universe. All life within the cosmos, the divine and the mundane is contained within his mouth. No doubt Yashoda's illusions were dissolved as she experienced this wonder.

This atomic technology, like the entity discussed in this book, is transmoral, not inherently evil. Rather it is the use to which it is put that causes the problem. Is this the fault of the Devil? To think so is to relieve ourselves of responsibility for our own actions or, more accurately, the actions of our leaders. If anything, our deployment of technological wonders shows that the more we advance, the more dangerous we become to ourselves and to the planet.

Revisiting the story of the birth of Oisín through the prism of the trickster-culture changer reveals a new layer to the supposed motivations of the Fear Dubh. Through his actions, Fionn and Sadhbh conceive the poet Oisín, who returns to fairyland and eventually ends up in the time of St. Patrick. Through his debates with St. Patrick he gives a good account of himself, and challenges the dogma of the Saint. In the written records of the monks the Dark Man places himself in one of the great Irish myths, where we recognize him centuries later. He is not the central figure of the story; he is the dark and mysterious figure in the background, pulling our strings and like marionettes . . .

we dance

. . . and he laughs.

And sometimes we lose our children.

6

The Dark Womb and Rewilding the Soul

The first story enacts a struggle between two peoples who have chosen two different ways of being in the world. The Fomorians have chosen to shape nature to suit them. Surrendering to it, the Tuatha Dé Danann have chosen to let nature shape them to suit it. Our way now is wholly Fomorian. It isn't working, or, rather, it has proved to be utterly disastrous; so it is that back out over nine waves and, wiser now we hope, we go we come back into an alternative experience of ourselves in a world alternatively experienced.

JOHN MORIARTY ON *THE LEBOR GABÁLA*
(THE BOOK OF INVASIONS)

Our first temples were caves. Deep wombs within the earth. Our ancestors lived and died in them. Inspired by the creative impulse, they crawled through the dark tunnels of the underworld to paint scenes of hunting, to leave stencil handprints on the walls as if to say, "I am alive." Among these scenes there are other beings depicted: half human, half animal, antlered and horned beings. These therianthropic figures adorn caves throughout the world.

The Cave of the Trois-Frères in Ariège, southwestern France, is home to one such piece of cave art entitled the *Sorcerer*, which is dated to approximately 13,000 BC. A composite figure, the being has been interpreted as having antlers, bear paws, and owl eyes. Henri Breuil, a French Catholic priest, archaeologist, anthropologist, and geologist who studied cave art and made sketches of the *Sorcerer* (which were published in the 1920s), theorized that the figure depicted a shaman. Author Margaret Murry believed it was "the first depiction of a deity on Earth."[1] More modern photographs failed to reveal significant details depicted by Breuil, and raised the critique that perhaps Breuil misinterpreted the cracks and contours of the cave wall to be part of the original work. Prehistorian Jean Clottes believed Breuil's drawing to be accurate:

> Breuil's drawing is quite honest and admitted by all the specialists who have seen the so-called Sorcerer in the cave (I have seen it myself perhaps 20 times over the years and I can assure you that it is very well preserved and genuine).[2]

In Dordogne, France, over two hundred engravings, mostly of animals, are found in the cave Grotte de Gabillou. One engraving of particular note, also known as *The Sorcerer*, depicts a horned, animal-headed figure with a beard and rear legs and bent so as to suggest they are those of a human being, replete with a human foot. Margaret Murry's assertion speculates that these ancient works provide an unbroken thread of belief to later horned gods such as Cernunnos or Herne. But this is lost in time—we cannot know. I do think this art suggests that a significant power has always been with us, demanding expression. The cave was clearly a sacred space for our ancestors, perhaps seen as an entrance to the underworld or land of the dead. And the Dark Man, often horned and hoofed, has always watched from the shadows, whispering to his children.

European descendants of these cave artists replicated the cave in their passage tombs and cairns. The most notable tombs in Ireland are at Newgrange, Knowth, and Dowth of the Boyne valley. On the winter solstice, the rising sun enters the chamber of Newgrange, and

Fig. 5. Henri Breuil's sketch of the *Sorcerer.*
Wikimedia Commons

at sunset it enters the chamber of Dowth. The solar phallus enters the vulva of the earth, impregnating it for life to begin again after the death of winter's lowest point. To the pre-Christian Irish, Ireland was a living goddess embodied in the landscape, and its glens and caves her vulva. The most evident example of this embodiment of the land is the Paps of Anu, a pair of breast-shaped mountains in County Kerry. Christianity's virgin birth to a celibate god severed copulation from female sexuality in particular, removing it from its rightful place of veneration to a place of revulsion and fear. This tragedy led to the desacralization of the earth which, combined with monotheism and the demonization of the Dark Man, is catastrophic. Human beings become separate from nature and we, like the Fomorians, are given license to shape nature to suit ourselves. Thus the vulva cave became the hellmouth, changing from a source of wonder and the threshold of creation to a place of corruption and spiritual danger. Nature, no longer sacred, becomes our subordinate, and its soul is demonized. Worse still, we now shape our bodies to the empty artifice of technology as we are hollowed out of meaning by modernity. Our backs are office-hunched, our shoulders rounded. We once watched the flight of migrating birds in search of auguries. Now we watch trending feeds on Twitter, a feed that offers no nourishment. Eyes that once scanned the sea's horizon no longer look up from a phone. We have utterly abandoned the natural world.

The cave-as-vulva suggests a womb within, replete with life-giving waters. The otherworldly source of Ireland's rivers is Connla's Well. It is surrounded by nine hazel trees, the same magic wood from which the Fear Dubh made his wand. The well represents a primordial dark womb, the spring of life and inspiration. It is a womb of making and unmaking. It is the source of Ireland's great river Shannon and the river Boyne.

> There is a singular myth which, while intended to account for the name of the River Shannon, expresses the Celtic veneration for poetry and science, combined with the warning that they may not be approached without danger. The goddess Sinend, it was said, daughter of Lodan son of Lir, went to a certain well named Connla's Well, which is under the sea—i.e., in the Land of Youth in Fairyland. "That is a well," says the bardic narrative, "at which are the hazels of wisdom and inspirations, that is, the hazels of the science of poetry, and in the same hour their fruit and their blossom and their foliage break forth, and then fall upon the well in the same shower, which raises upon the water a royal surge of purple." When Sinend came to the well we are not told what rites or preparation she had omitted, but the angry waters broke forth and overwhelmed her, and washed her up on the Shannon shore, where she died, giving to the river its

name. This myth of the hazels of inspiration and knowledge and their association with springing water runs through all Irish legend, and has been finely treated by a living Irish poet, Mr. G. W. Russell, in the following verses . . .

> *And when the sun sets dimmed in eve, and purple fills the air,*
> *I think the sacred hazel-tree is dropping berries there,*
> *From starry fruitage, waved aloft where Connla's Well o'erflows;*
> *For sure, the immortal waters run through every wind that blows.*[3]

Similarly the river Boyne is named for the Goddess Boann, who approached the well and circled it widdershins (anti-clockwise) despite the warnings of her husband, Nechtan. The well's waters rose up and swept away the goddess, taking from her an eye, an arm, and a leg before she succumbed to the waters. The river Boyne was created in this process. Here it is described in *The Metrical Dindshenchas*:

> *Therefore none of them dared approach it*
> *save Nechtain and his cup-bearers:*
> *these are their names, famed for brilliant deed,*
> *Flesc and Lam and Luam.*
>
> *Hither came on a day white Boand*
> *(her noble pride uplifted her),*
> *to the never-failing well to make trial of its power.*
> *As thrice she walked round*
> *about the well heedlessly, three waves burst from it,*
> *whence came the death of Boand.*
>
> *They came each wave of them against a limb,*
> *they disfigured the soft-blooming woman:*
> *a wave against her foot, a wave against her perfect eye,*
> *the third wave shatters one hand.*

She rushed to the sea (it was better for her)
to escape her blemish,
so that none might see her mutilation;
on herself fell her reproach.

Every way the woman went
the cold white water followed
from the Sid to the sea (not weak it was)
So that thence it is called Boand.[4]

The fates of the two goddesses who gave their names to the great rivers serve as a warning regarding the pursuit of knowledge. To approach the otherworldly well and learn its secrets without the necessary guides was to court doom, even for a goddess. It was under the protection of dark magic.

Connla's well, loud was its sound,
was beneath the blue-skirted ocean:
six streams, unequal in fame,
rise from it, the seventh was Sinann.

The nine hazels of Crimall the sage
drop their fruits yonder under the well:
they stand by the power of magic spells
under a darksome mist of wizardry.[5]

From each hazel tree a windfallen nut fell into its water. Encased within a hard shell, each nut contained a portion of the world's knowledge. In Connla's Well, there lived a salmon that swallowed a hazelnut from each tree. The knowledge contained therein was imparted into the flesh of the salmon. It became the Salmon of Knowledge, the embodiment of all gnosis.

In its bones it held the songs of the world.
In its pink flesh the knowledge of atom and archon.
In its shining scales the map of the universe.
Betwixt its dorsal spines, cosine and sine.

In its heart the arts of love and war.
In its eyes the world's birth and death.
In its tail the poet's wit and rhymer's skill.
Betwixt its gills flowed time and dreamtime.

The salmon traveled through the waters of the otherworld to Ireland, its perfect form gliding between worlds. Tuan mac Cairill came to Ireland as before the flood, retaining the memories of his centuries of dream lives as Irish totem animals. Incarnated as a salmon, he was eaten by the Queen of Ulster who became pregnant and gave birth to Tuan the human.

Like the *Sorcerer* on the cave wall in France, he is a composite being of fin, wing, tusk, and antler.

I had been a man, a stag, a boar, a bird, and now I was a fish. In all my changes I had joy and fulness of life. But in the water joy lay deeper, life pulsed deeper. For on land or air there is always something hindering. The stage has legs to be tucked away for sleep, and untucked for movement; and the bird has wings that must be folded and pecked and cared for. But the fish has but one piece from his nose to his tail. He is complete, single and unencumbered.[6]

Tuan's story is important in that it represents a restoration of right relation with a living cosmos by removing our separation from it and defeating duality. His spirit experiences Ireland in multiple animal forms before being born in the womb of the ocean and then ingested into the womb of woman. It is a reminder of our true self and the nature of our experience. British geographer and archaeologist Michael Dames, in his book *Mythic Ireland*, reflects on Tuan:

Only by empathising with, and thus becoming, the "lower" species can humanity hope to return from spiritual, moral and physical death.[7]

This context is important, considering the shape-shifting accounts of witches. Did the experience of being in another living thing's form in vision or otherwise serve to rewild the mind and position the witch alongside the animal world rather than above it? Like the *Sorcerer's* composite body and the Dark Man's shape-shifting, it implicitly denies our partition from nature. It is in direct opposition to Christian separation.

Just as the Tuatha Dé Danann shaped themselves to suit the natural world, the wisdom and inspiration of the otherworld was embodied in Salmon form. As the *vesica piscis*, the Salmon of Knowledge, the curved, living jewel, left the mystical waters of Connla's Well for the river Boyne where it was fated the poet Finegas would catch the fish. Finegas was accompanied by a boy he had taken into his service. It is young Fionn mac Cumhaill who, in order to hide from his enemies, has called himself Deimne. Finegas catches the divine fish and leaves it with Fionn to prepare with the instruction not to eat any of its flesh. On the poet's return, he asks the noble boy if he had tasted the fish, to which he replies he had tasted it by chance. While the fish was roasting a great blister rose on its skin. Fionn pressed it down, and in the process, he burnt his thumb, which he placed in his mouth to soothe. On hearing this, Finegas tells Fionn the full prophecy of the fish's capture—he would catch the fish but not eat it—and he called the boy by his true name.

> "It was given to you," Finegas answered. "Fionn, the son of Uail, the son of Baiscne, and it will be given to him."
>
> "You shall have a half of the fish," cried Fionn.
>
> "I will not eat a piece of its skin that is as small as the point of its smallest bone," said the resolute and trembling bard. "Let you now

eat up the fish, and I shall watch you and give praise to the gods of the Underworld and of the Elements."[8]

Finegas tells us the nature of knowledge within the divine fish and the true nature of Connla's Well.

> Fionn then ate the Salmon of Knowledge, and when it had disappeared a great jollity and tranquility and exuberance returned to the poet.
> "Ah," said he, "I had a great combat with that fish."
> "Did it fight for its life?" Fionn inquired.
> "It did, but that was not the fight I meant."[9]

The fight was his internal battle to adhere to his fate and not eat the fish, which contained the knowledge and inspiration he so desired. He is deeply challenged by this fight, but self-mastery prevails, and the fish is placed in the hands of Fionn, fulfilling the prophecy.

Folklore helps us understand and map the *other-scape*, the landscape of the otherworld that intersects with our dreams. It is crucial to understanding our place in the spiritual landscape of the planet. The Dark Man guides us through the cave to the Dark Womb within. Once you have been tapped on the shoulder by him it is only a matter of time before you stand on the edge of the cold furnace of creation, the fecund water of the Dark Womb. Hereditary witch Shullie H. Porter, whose interview appears in part two of this book, describes visiting the womb:

> *I've had "the Crona" again, only this time worse . . . and was high in fever. It knocked me for six. As I lay in bed, in the midst of it, and feeling very, very ill and sorry for myself, the atmosphere of the room changed and I heard my heart stop. Just stop. Nothing, no pulse, no sound, no big bang, just stopped, and it all went very, very, very quiet. I lay there and thought "Oh, so I'm dead . . ." Just like that.*

Then Our Man came, and I looked to him and said to him, "I'm dead, then?" He asked me if it mattered. I said, "Yes, I don't really want to go, not yet." I was so calm, very calm. It felt like it did when I drowned years ago, and when he came to me when my femoral artery popped. The first time he opened the door, and I went to the desert with him. It was like that and so peaceful and calm. I had no qualms for in that moment, that instant of time, I really did think I was actually dead.

After I said I didn't want to go yet, he nodded, and didn't say anything more but bent down, with his big arms, a hint of a wing, picked me up. Like a child. He took me down to the cave I have told you about and to the bottomless black rock pool that is there. I told him as I looked at it, that I was afraid I'd sink if he put me in there as, "it's bottomless, the clue is in the name." He laughed. The water was a dark black, like a black hole kind of black, like his face can be, but with a green hue to it, as if a green light was coming up from below. Despite my somewhat reluctance, he placed me gently and carefully in it; the water enveloped me, but I floated and didn't sink, much to my relief. He told me to sleep, as I drifted away into the middle of this pool which now seemed vast, oceans vast yet still a pool in a cave. I started to float into "sleep." After what seemed like an age, I started to hear my blood pumping, though my heart itself was still quiet. The blood started to make that whooshing sound it does, and I remember being surprised and then suddenly I heard my heart start to beat again, really, really loudly, like it was echoing in the cave. I woke up. I was, as you can expect, surprised to be in my bed and covered in sweat. Oh, and extremely thirsty. The fever had not so much broken, but I knew I was over the worse.

I too have been to the Dark Womb in meditation. The womb will reveal to you what is necessary. It is part of the void and also part of the place of creation. Like the Dark Man who is the guardian of its mysteries, it will appear to you as an expression of what is in your heart. I do not know what this place truly is, no more than I know what the Dark Man is. I only know my experience, and what it showed me. As Shullie described, it was infinite yet still a pool. It was cold but forgiving, still but ceaseless, an amniotic ocean from the earth's birth. It is from this sacred water the Salmon of Knowledge swam to the river Boyne.

Like Tuan, we have all been once a stag, a boar, a hawk, and a salmon. The Dark Man shows us there is no separation, that duality is an illusion. The other-scape is the landscape but you must rewild yourself to see it. John Moriarty once spoke of seeing a hare bolt out in front of him as he walked across the bog. The hare left an impression of its body in the heather where it had been resting. He dropped down and placed his head into that impression, still warm from the hare's body and filled with its scent. As he lay there, he asked the hare and the wild grasses to draw all the European learning and mind out of him, like a poultice. He pushed his head down into the form, like a womb, but this time a womb of unmaking, not a womb of making, so he may rewild himself, to have an unencumbered form like the salmon.

> *Let us lie down and place our heads in the hare's bed.*
> *Let us pick the Salmon's bones clean.*
> *Let us see with new eyes the other-scape abound.*
> *Let us awaken the stag, the boar, the hawk and the*
>   *salmon within.*
> *Let our Gods and Goddesses consummate their passion.*
> *Let the Dark One lead us in the crossroads dance.*
> *Let him ignite the fire in our blood.*
> *Let us be wild once more and sing.*

As witches and storytellers, the wild spirits call to us and initiate the process of rewilding our souls. It is up to us to finish it, to leave our handprint on the cave wall and say:

I do not merely exist. I am not a hollow being.

I

Am

Alive.

7

Confessions of Witches

There was an old woman and she lived in the woods
Weila Weila Waile
There was an old woman and she lived in the woods
Down by the river Saile.

"WEILA WAILE" BY THE DUBLINERS

As with the djinn and the fairies, modern American culture has largely defanged the meaning of being a witch and practicing witchcraft. The Leannán Sídhe became Tinkerbell; the Ifrit became Aladdin's singing genie; so, too, the witch has been sanitized. There were very good reasons to fear the witch. It was after all the ultimate "other": part wild, dangerous, with fire in the blood. Equally the witch served a purpose as an intermediary between the otherworld forces that butted up against the rural communities. The witch could remove fairy maleficence but equally could be the vehicle for its delivery. Romanticizing the pastoral life of the early modern British and Irish peasant is disingenuous; life as a subsistence farmer was brutal and hung on a knife edge between serfdom and starvation. These communities hedged their bets and prayed to God for salvation and to the Devil for survival. The death or illness of a key family member could condemn the survivors to destitution and death. It was against this desperate background the Dark Man or an emissary often made an appearance, with the offer of a deal.

Mediation with the forces of chaos is not without danger or

consequences. In sixteenth- and seventeenth-century Britain, the dominant socioreligious structures set out to persecute the witches, framing them as a spiritual fifth column. In Scotland an estimated 1,500 people, mostly women, were strangled and then burned for witchcraft.[1] Far more were tried. The subsequent records from these trials and those in England have provided us with a window into their beliefs and practices. This comes with its own challenges, not least as Peter Grey points out in *Apocalyptic Witchcraft*, "most of our history is chronicled by our enemies."[2]

The same stands for our folklore. Our stories are full of symbolic victories of the church over the fairy world, from the church bells driving the fairies away to the Lord's Prayer undoing fairy maleficence. The confessions extracted from the witches are responses to questions asked from a Christian perspective and are recorded as such. This Christian framework is one that must be acknowledged as we read the words attributed to the witches. That said, the patterns of the Dark Man identified in the folklore are abundantly present in the confession materials. The witches' confessions could be dismissed as the words of desperate women telling their inquisitors what they want to hear, if it were not for the consistencies. There are accounts across Britain—from Somerset to Scotland—that present consistencies with both folklore and the experience of modern witches.

The Survey of Scottish Witchcraft[3] is a superb resource for the history of witchcraft and witch hunting in Scotland. Nearly 4,000 individuals—all of whom are known to have been accused of witchcraft in early modern Scotland—are included in the database. There is information on where and when they were accused, how they were tried, their testimonies, and what happened to them. The Dark Man is not universally present in these records. But there are dozens of accounts featuring a figure matching his description. Yet again, a pattern emerges.

Margaret Alexander, tried in 1647, referred to a man in black clothes who "made her go forward." She also spoke of a man being the "King of the Fairies" who she had sex with. When pressed, she described his physical nature as cold. Her fate is unknown.[4] Margaret Allan, tried in 1661, had a servant testify they saw a black man go into Margaret's room and appear to move around like he had hooves. Margaret was banished.[5] Thomas Black, tried in 1661, said the Devil appeared to him at night while he was in bed. He went on to describe the Devil lying upon him heavily, in the shape of a man. Thomas was executed by strangulation and burned.[6] Agnes Clarkson was tried in 1649 and spoke of how her home was filled with a black mist when she first refused to join the Devil. When questioned as to how she renounced her baptism, she explained this was done through carnal dealings with the Dark Man. Her fate is unknown.[7] Margret Jackson, tried in 1677, described the Devil as a black man with a bluish band, white cuffs, and hogers (leg coverings). He wore no shoes and had cloven feet. She was visited in bed by a spirit that looked like her dead husband, but she later realized it was the Devil.[8] This is reminiscent of how Sadhbh was tricked by the Dark Man when he appears as Fionn. Margret was executed by strangulation and burned. Widow Christian Patersone, tried in 1661, said the Devil changed from a beast to a man to get into bed with her. She gave a detailed account of sex with him. Christian was executed by strangulation and burned.[9]

And of course there is the most famous Scottish account of all, that of Isobel Gowdie, in 1662. Her vivid and lurid confession is startling in its detail. The Devil baptized her with blood he sucked from her Devil's mark, spat it in her hand and sprinkled it over her head. His carnal nature was cold. He felt like ice-cold spring water inside her when they had sex. She described the Devil's penis as immense and that the younger women of the coven took more pleasure in sex with the Devil than with their husbands. The Devil also beat them at meetings, and they would never refuse his advances.

Isobel's confession is astonishing in its own right but even more so when mapped across British and Irish folklore. Using the confessions as the primary source materials, I will focus on five key areas:

- The dark appearance and appellation
- Appearance as a composite being
- Shape-shifting
- Interceptor and trickster nature
- Sex and sexual interest in human beings

Historian Emma Wilby has provided us with a rich interdisciplinary work on Isobel's case in her superb book *The Visions of Isobel Gowdie: Magic, Witchcraft and Dark Shamanism in Seventeenth-Century Scotland*. Including facsimiles of the original trial records, it is a comprehensive and fair-minded thesis on the subject.

Isobel confessed to witchcraft at Auldearn in Scotland in 1662, making four confessions over a six-week period. It's unknown what happened to her. The following text is from her first confession (following Emma Wilby's work, spelling and punctuation are exactly as found in the documents. Shorthand omissions are noted in square parentheses):

> . . . as I wes goeing betuixt the townes of drumdewin and the headis: I met w[i]th the divell and ther coventanted in a maner w[i]th him, and I promeisit to meit him in the night tym in the kirk of aulderne q[uhi]lk I did: and the first thing I did ther th[a]t night I denyed my baptisme, and did put the on of my handis to the crowne of my head and the uth[e]r to the sole of my foot, and th[e]n renuncet all betwixt my two handis ower to the divell, he wes in the readeris dask and a blak book in his hand: margret brodie in aulderne held me vp to the divell to be baptized be him, and he marked me in the showlder, and suked owt my blood at that merk and spowted it in his hand, and sprinkling it on my head said I baptise the Janet in my awin name, and w[i]thin a q[uhi]ll we all remoowed . . .[10]

Isobel recounts her meeting with the Devil as she was traveling. Note, her journey is interrupted by him in the space outside of the town. She is intercepted, just as Mr. Kirwan was with Finvarra and Jemmy Nowlan with the Dark Horseman. In their conversation she agrees to meet him at the Church of Aulderne where she is baptized by him in blood, renouncing Christianity and giving herself to him.

> . . . the nixt tym th[a]t I met w[i]th him ves in the new wardis of Inshoch, and haid carnall cowpula[tio]n & dealling w[i]th me, he wes a meikle blak roch man werie cold and I faund his nature als cold w[i]thin me as spring wall vater somtymes he haid buitis & somtymes shoes on his foot bot still his foot ar forked and cloven he vold be somtymes w[i]th ws lyk a dear or a rae . . .[11]

Here Isobel describes her next meeting with the Devil, calling him a "meikle blak roch man," meaning a "great black rough man." Throughout the confessions he is referred to as the Devil and variants of meikle blak man. In confession three, Isobel mentions that among themselves the coven members called him "blak jon." The color black is used not only as a descriptor but as an appellation, just as with Fear Dorcha, Fear Dubh, and Donn Dubh. Isobel says he had sex with her and he felt cold as spring water within her. Finally, she says that sometimes he had boots or shoes, and he had cloven feet. Then she adds a detail that is astonishing. She describes that he would sometimes be like a deer or a "rae." She describes both his shape-shifting and composite nature, connecting him to the shape-shifting deer women in the stories of the Fear Dubh and Donn Dubh. At first glance this may appear as the opposite to what occurs in the mythology but, as Joshua Cutchin describes in *Ecology of Souls*:

> Inversion equals representation in these stories. Seemingly oppositional motifs often share a root source. For example, the faeries are ever-leaving, extraterrestrials ever-arriving in their respective folklore.[12]

In Isobel's third confession, there is further detail regarding sexual intercourse:

> . . . and ther haid carnall cowpula[tio]n w[i]th me, he wes a werie
> meikle blak roch man, he will lye als hewie wpon ws q[uhe]n he
> hes carnall dealling w[i]th us, als lyk an malt secke; his memberis ar
> exceiding great and long, no mans memberis ar so long and bigg as
> they ar: he wold be amongst us, lyke a weath horse amongst mearis
> he wold lye w[i]th ws in p[rese]nce of all the multitud, neither haid
> we nor he any kynd of shame, bot especiallie he hes no sham w[i]th
> him at all, he wold lye and haw carnall dealling w[i]th all enyie tym
> as he pleased, he wold haw carnall dealling w[i]th us in the shape
> of a deir or any uth[e]r shap th[a]t he wold be in, we wold never
> refuse him. he wold com to my hows top in the shape of a crow, or
> lyk a dear or in any uther shap now and then, I wold ken his voice
> at the first heiring of it, and wold goe furth to him and hav carnall
> cowpula[tio]n w[i]th him . . . The yowngest and lustiest woomen
> will haw werie great pleasur in their carnall cowpula[tio]n w[i]th
> him, yea much mor th[a]n w[i]th their awin husbandis, and they
> will haw a exceiding great desyr of it w[i]th him, als much as he can
> haw to them & mor, and never think shame of it, he is able for ws
> th[a]t way th[a]n any man can be, (alace th[a]t I sould compare him
> to an man) onlie he ves heavie lyk a malt seck a hodg nature, verie
> cold as yce.[13]

Again there is the description of the Dark Man: he is noted as being
as heavy as a malt sack when he lies upon the women of the coven, and
his penis was immense. He would go from witch to witch like a stallion
among mares in front of everyone and there was no shame experienced
by the participants. Sometimes he would copulate with the witches in
the form of a deer or other forms, and they would never refuse him. He
would come to Isobel's house in the form of a deer, and she would recognize his voice. In confession three, she describes him in further forms:

Somtym he vold be lyk a stirk, a bull, a deir, a rae, or a dowg etc and haw dealling w[i]tj ws.[14]

The youngest and lustiest women took more pleasure in sex with the Dark Man than they did with their own husbands. The description of how the witches enjoyed overwhelming pleasure with the Dark Man is akin to the overwhelming lust and love Fionn immediately felt for Sadhbh, who came to him originally in the form of a deer. This union between the wild and human worlds is hinted at in the symbolic marriage between girl and puck goat during the Puck Fair in Ireland. Isobel's description of the libidinous Dark Man could be mistaken for the god Pan in his prouder depictions. Richard Payne Knight discussed Pan in his *Discourse on the Worship of Priapus* (1786) as a symbol of creation expressed through sexuality. I believe this is an aspect of mystery surrounding the Dark Man and his interaction with witches. The sex experienced by Isobel and her coven is in itself a rite in honor of creation.

The *Dictionnaire Infernal* by Jacques Collin de Plancy is a list of demons organized into hierarchies and attributes and by the descriptions of their manifestations. It was first published in 1818 and republished in 1863, featuring sixty-nine illustrations depicting the demons by Louis Le Breton. There is a description of a demon called Master Leonard. He is a composite, having three horns, two fox-like ears, and a goat's beard—harking back to the *Sorcerer* of Trois-Frère cave—and he presides over the sabbath in the form of a goat from the waist up.

Leonard, demon of the first order, grand master of the sabbaths, chief of the subaltern demons, inspector general of sorcery, black magic, and the witches. He is often called "le Gran Negre" (the Black Man).[15]

Another source on Master Leonard is *Dogme et Rituel de la Haute Magie Part II: The Ritual of Transcendental Magic* by Eliphas Levi, a text published in 1896. The text bears a remarkable likeness to the accounts of Isobel Gowdie.

> To Sabbaths dreamed in this manner we must refer the accounts of a goat issuing from pitchers and going back into them after the ceremony; infernal powders obtained from the ordure of this goat, who is called Master Leonard; banquets where abortions are eaten without salt and boiled with serpents and toads; dances, in which monstrous animals or men and women with impossible shapes take part; unbridled debauches where incubi project cold sperm.[16]

The pattern and attributes of the Dark Man are very similar. Further to that the detail on "cold sperm" is so specific it is hard to conceive that Levi and Gowdie are not describing the same entity. Could it be the incubi's "cold sperm" was the reason the Dark Man felt as cold as spring water within the female witches he lay with?

Isobel and the coven carried out mischief and malefica in the Devil's name, acting as the Trickster's agents: "q[uhe]n ve goe to any hous we tak meat and drink, and we fill wp the barrellis w[i]th owr oven pish again."[17] Isobel describes how they would go from house to house eating and drinking their fill and then refilling the empty beer or ale barrels with their urine.

> . . . whan we tak away any cowes milk we pull the taw and twyn it & plaitt it the vrong way in the divellis name, and we draw the tedder (sua maid) in betuixt the coves hinder foot and owt betuixt the cowes forder foot, in the divellis namn and therby tak w[i]th ws the kowes milk, we tak sheips milk ewin so.[18]

Isobel describes how she and her coven members would create a witch's ladder by making a tether of the cow's hair plaited the wrong way in the Devil's name, using it to steal the cow's milk, and doing the same with sheep.

q[uhe]n ve tak away the strenth of anie persones eall giwes it to an uth[e]t we tak a litle qwantitie owt of each barrell or stan (stand?) of & puts it in a stowp, in the divellis nam, and in his nam w[i]th owr awin handis putts it in amongst an uth(e)ris eall and giwes hir the strenth and substance & seall of hir neightbo[u]ris eall.[19]

Not only did they replace their neighbor's ale with urine, they would steal the "strength" from a person's ale and give it to another: a deeply unwise course of action to take in Scotland. Far more troubling was the coven's random killing of people with elf arrows:

we haw no bow to shoot w[i]th bot spang them from of the naillis of owr thowmbes: som tymes we will miss bot if they twitch be it beast or man or woman it will kill tho they had an Jack upon them![20]

The witches shot arrows under the instruction of the devil, who told them to go out and kill in his name. The arrows were shot from the witches' thumbs, and they were lethal. If they struck home, they would kill—beast or man or woman. Even wearing armor would not protect the victims.

Isobel recounts shape-shifting into various animal forms such as cats, hares, or crows on several occasions. She describes this transformation, or "turnskin," taking place instantaneously and with ease:

Qwhen we goe in the shape of an haire, we say thryse ower I sall gow intill a haire w[i]th sorrow and syt and meikle caire, and I sall goe in the divellis nam ay whill I com hom (damaged—words missing) (in?)stantlie we start in an hair, and when we wold be owt of th[a]t shape we vill s . . . (damaged—words missing) caire, I am in an hairis liknes just now, bot I salbe in a womans liknes ew . . . (damaged— words missing) when we vold goe in the liknes of an cat: we say thryse ower I sall goe int(ill?) (damaged—words missing) shot, and

I sall goe in the divellis nam, ay q[uhi]ll I com hom again:, & if ve
(damaged—words missing) we say thryse ower I sall goe intill a craw
w[i]th sorrow and syt & blak (damaged—words missing) ay q[uhi]
ll I com home again: and q[uhe]n ve vold be owt of thes shapes, we
say: catt cat (damaged—words missing) send the a blak shott or blak
thraw: I wes a catt or crow just now, bot I salbe (damaged—words
missing) catt: catt: or craw: craw: goe send the a blak shot or a blak
thraw.[21]

The theme of shape-shifting is repeatedly seen in folklore featuring
variants of the Dark Man. We know from the story of Tuan mac Cairill
and his many lives as the totem animals of Ireland that there is deep
meaning within the concept of shape-shifting. It infers we are not separate or individual from the animal world. The modern-day traditional
witch also experiences this shape-shifting. It is the natural world, the
land, absorbing one into its consciousness, dissolving us into an animal
form. Robert Artisson, in *The Horn of Evenwood*, considers the slippery
nature of the Dark Man's shape-shifting.

The Witchfather has existed in every era of human history, and in
the countless eras before that. He's been worshipped as God, feared
as a devil, and sought by the wise in thousands of forms and disguises. For all that, he can't rightly be called a God, an angel, a devil,
a spirit, or a man. Sure, he is those things, depending on who you
ask, but he's also none of those things. If you try to catch him, you'll
find that it's impossible.

This is because he's a Turnskin, a master shape-shifter, who has
no "native" form which can be caught. One of his greatest tricks
is to slip out of any net, any trap, even the traps of death and
mortality.[22]

The composite nature of the Dark Man and the shape-shifting of the
witches all point to nondualism and a rejection of our separation.

If you are any one thing in particular, you can be trapped. He wants you to shed your skin like one of his favorite disguises, the serpent, and slither beyond the snares of delusion.[23]

Whatever we decide we are, we become. That is the trap. As fairy gold turns to dead leaves, our words spin illusions around us that limit our perspective and potential. Tuan mac Cairill dreamed himself a new form as another met its end. Each form fell beneath tooth and claw until, as the unencumbered salmon, he was netted, setting the events in motion that would return him to human form. Unlike Tuan, the Dark Man is forever formless and ever shifting and can never be netted.

PART II

◇ ◇ ◇

Witnesses and Witches

8

Elise Oursa, Blood & Ink

Elise Oursa is a card reader, artist, a practicing witch, and creator of The Blood & Ink Tarot. I'm very proud to call her a friend. She has been an invaluable colleague and fellow explorer into the world of the Dark Man. Her witchcraft is largely solitary and spirit-based and has evolved through her experience as a therapist. She is guided by her work with Hekate, her connection to the chthonic currents of the British landscape, and a deep reverence for those who have come before. She teaches on the tarot and designs bespoke rituals for transformation and empowerment.

I feel a particular affinity for Elise's story because it was through our conversations that the foundational investigations into the subject matter of this book came to light. Elise had never heard of the *Fear Dubh* or *The Black Magician of the Men of God*. Yet the name of one of the main characters in the stories explained in chapter 2 was repeated to her in her dreams. For me this was when folklore and witchcraft became irrevocably intertwined and the Dark Man went from being an interesting folkloric theme to something far more potent.

◆ ◆ ◆

Elise Oursa

I was engaged in this encounter before I recognized that it was an encounter with a dark man, because I sat down in February 2020 and I made the decision to rapidly create a Tarot deck. And from the

Fig. 6. *Roy du Pique*—King of Spades from the Blood & Ink tarot deck.
By Elise Oursa

ROY DE PIQUE

moment I started putting paint to paper, I was just kind of overtaken in this energy that was moving through me. And it was very clear to me that this was coming from somewhere that was beyond me. And the Tarot deck came forth over a weekend for the major arcana, and then maybe two weeks for the second half of the deck, for the minor arcana, so very quickly. And it was just this incredible feeling of this force moving through me creatively, which was probably much bigger than my physicality was prepared for! Some of the images of the deck are quite dark. There's a lot of shadow, personal shadow in the images and in the cards as well. It's not an airy-fairy new age piece of work, it's pretty hard core, that came through me. And the day after

I finished it, I was wrecked—physically, emotionally, and mentally—after producing this huge body of work. And I had a dream—and I quite often have these kinds of prophetic dreams—well, more like spirit contact dreams, where it's very clear that I need to be in that dream space to have that sort of spirit contact. And in this space, in this dream, there was a dark man standing next to my bed, and he said to me, "Okay, now you've finished the job—it's a Grimoire—you need to go off and figure out how to use it." I associated that dark man beside the bed with, in particular, three of the cards that are in the deck. One, of course, was the devil. One was the King of Swords. The image for the King of Swords is a very dashing gentleman in his topcoat with his hat and almost a plague doctor mask, but it could be a crow as well. And bear in mind that these were created just before the pandemic hit, I mean, literally a week or two before Covid hit. So I think that image in itself was quite prophetic of what was to come. So that was the first interaction with this figure. And then I started working with the cards. I had all this art, this paper, to work with, so I started working with them in ritual and in vision, and at that point I didn't have clarity on what he had meant by "It's a Grimoire." It wasn't like I was then given particular spells or things like that to add into it as a body of work. It was more that it just opened a series of connections and synchronicities that started to unfold and are continually unfolding. So I decided to publish the major arcana deck and release that as a talismanic magical object. And it took me until the following February, like a complete year, to get this going because we were in Covid times at this time and everything's going on. So I wasn't quick off the ball with that. But when I made that decision to release the major arcana deck, that's when things really started heating up.

One of the things was that another dream came to me. And in this dream, instead of the dark man, there was a dark woman standing beside the bed. And I have a very vivid memory of how she was dressed. She had a veil and this dress on that was almost made of feathers. But I think in general she looked like the Cailleach or the Morrigan or something like that. She gave me her name. And it was one of these dreams where she was just repeating in my ear, whispering her name over and over and over and over again so that I wouldn't forget it when I woke up. And the name (was given) really slowly, very vividly: Sadhbh, Sadhbh. So I woke up remembering that name, wrote it down, and had no clue what it was. I went off googling. And of course I'm spelling it as I heard it, like a normal English-speaking person! And then, I guess, came the synchronicity. Of course, over that year I've met you, I've met other people coming with these sorts of experiences from different directions. And you put me onto this story about Fear Dorcha, the dark man from Irish mythology. And I started to look at reading some of the stories about that. And then I discovered that his abducted wife—in folklore—was Sadhbh. I thought, okay, it was a dark man. It's a devil figure. It's the dark man at the crossroads. We're dealing with some underworld energy here. And coming from witchcraft practice, that sort of delighted me on many levels, because it's really like the initiation. I'm big into that, into owning our underworld places. So that was resonant with where I am in my practice. But then when I received that name, I was like, okay, wow, there's something more here. I don't have Irish heritage at all, I'm not familiar with Irish mythology, although I am very connected to the British landscape and this is my ancestral home. And that really opened up this path to looking at the connection to fairy. And I've always worked with land, with the forest, with wild spaces. But I then started looking at and working with it in a different way, and as more as a response to the fairy element.

At the time the major arcana deck was produced, I did 100 copies: a limited edition. Each one was ritually charged. And even the specific steps with the ritual that I used, I feel were given to me. I was very aware of that presence of the dark man telling me exactly what to do to consecrate the decks and to set them really to his service, which sounds a bit Christian and creepy, but that's what it was. And *so it became clear to me that each of those 22 cards was a specific spirit that was inhabiting the space of the deck and the space of each card within the space of the system of the deck in itself. And the deck started selling. It started going out to people. And then these really fascinating and unnerving synchronicities started to happen. So people who received the deck started finding gifts left just outside their door, or they started receiving things that they hadn't ordered, like Amazon books, just various things. And it happened a few times. And it was like, okay, yeah, that's weird. But the thing that made the thread between all of these was everyone was receiving either magical tools or books that had to do with Irish folklore and mythology or Celtic folklore. So there were three or four people who did not order the book but received Caitlin Matthews's Art of Celtic Seership book. And for me, that was the thing: if you look at something with an oracular vision, I think you have to ask, okay, what is this thing doing? Books hold knowledge, that's what they do, or sometimes they hold secrets. But to receive a book about Celtic seership, it's a book that's specifically about paying attention to signs, and paying attention to signs that come from the landscape. And this seemed to be also tying back into the Celtic current again, which is, like I said, wasn't something that I'd consider doing with the deck because my Tarot practice is more like traditional Tarot de Marseille. A number of people found outside of their house incense and incense burners, just like the different tools and trade of doing magic. So it felt as if we were being given the instructions and the steps to do something with these decks. It got a bit wild! It's like ten or fifteen people that I know of within this cohort were experiencing this stuff.*

So from there, I took the deck and I created a ritual to create an Astral temple for the deck, which I created individually and then led I think about 60 people into the space in a visionary ritual. And after that, that space felt very solid. And there are people who have not been initiated into that space but have found it because they come to me after they've been working with the deck and they say,

"Hey, I saw this and this," and they have all those specific key points of what the space looks like—where it is, how it works, what you encounter there—and there's certain mechanics within that space as well. So people are finding it even without me guiding them into it, but specifically people who have worked with the deck. So I think that's been an important part of it as well, to create the tools with the deck and the opening to the signs and also the space, which then leads deeper and maybe leads more people into this experience of this relationship with the dark man figure.

Elise's account of being daimon-driven to the point of exhaustion to create art for the Dark Man is a scenario I'm familiar with. You're currently reading the results of my experience. Where my work is that of the storyteller, Elise's is that of the witch. The Blood & Ink deck are a received grimoire wherein the cards are portals. The cards also formed the center of a shared experience for those brought together from across the world to the Astral Temple and those who received magical tokens on their doorsteps.

The most remarkable part of this story for me is the naming of Sadhbh. While she is the mother of the great hero Oisín and lover to Fionn, she is a very transient figure in Irish mythology with only the briefest of cameos (and shorter cameos still while in human form). Essentially, she is a footnote in these epic tales. Although her impact has been felt for centuries, she is far from a central figure. The revealing of her name to Elise is simply astonishing, even more so when you realize she wasn't aware of the role Sadhbh played in the lore of the Dark Man.

Elise also describes being completely drained by her frantic production of the cards. This is the price the conduit pays. The price varies, from migraines to utter exhaustion. A lifetime of being a conduit, if unmanaged, can lead to far more devastating payments. Similarly, the Dark Man himself is not to be taken lightly under any circumstances. Not everyone makes it through the test of mettle unscathed. Elise wisely advocates caution.

I have reservations. I still see this as a witchcraft initiatory experience. I have concerns that people who are led into this, some of them might need more holding or might need more safety parameters. For me, it's not an easy energy. It's one that takes you face to face in confrontation with your shadow and with your darkness. And I think it's important that people like you—with the book that you're writing—and people like me who are guiding people into these spaces, for us not to sensationalize or make light of that darkness. You can't be an edgelord about it, because then that becomes egoic. That's not what it's about. It's a mindful integration that you're coming into contact with through this process.

Darragh Mason: *I think that's a really useful reflection. What happened after I had my visions was a breadcrumb trail of more information. The results made my digital space smaller and smaller as I had been given areas of focus to work on. And that's a direct result of these first experiences.*

Elise Oursa: *That's exactly what I can speak to. The direct results. I created the deck, and the pandemic hit, and then I set up my online community, Coffee and Cards, thinking it's just going to be like a hangout, reading some cards, drinking some coffee. And then it turned into kind of like the complete focus of everything—it's grown into a really vibrant and thriving and interesting online community without a lot of the drama that you find in other places, which is a blessing. That wouldn't have happened without the deck. We've been at that for two years now. Moving on from that, it's also just been a catalyst for my artistic practice. I hadn't done any art in years before I did the deck. I've just opened the floodgates to print. The deck is a set of monoprints. So that was my first experience of printmaking. But this last year, it's like the outside world has become much more static, focused for me. Like, now the thing I do is make art and run my community, which also facilitates the making of the art.*

I had Covid in February, and I went into that Covid experience whilst supporting someone else who felt they were under psychic or magical attack. I was very boundaried with how much I could support that person, but I was a bit concerned that this left me open to attack as well because I was really very ill. And while I was kind of in that sick haze, the dark man was there with me, as one of my cards: the King of Swords. When I was in and out of sleep, it was like he was wrapping me in his arm wings and just encasing me in protection while I slept. I felt like that was a whole other initiation into that energy as well. And we're talking about having contained focus in regards to our work and not having outside influence, and this was a manifestation of that. In witchcraft and magic and spell crafting, containment is a really important aspect. Whether it's your magic circle around you or the cauldron or the material for the spell, I think that there has to be a containment for your magic to grow. So I think maybe that's what you and I are both experiencing. It could really be that.

Darragh Mason: *You are very much an established witch, with experiences and knowledge in many different schools of magical thinking and magical practice. What do you think the Dark Man is?*

Elise Oursa: *I think the dark man is like a spirit of manifestation. I don't mean manifestation like "let me help you get a job." But a cosmic force of everything that comes into existence, is how I see it. And within that, it's necessary to have demiurgic forces: of structure and laws and rules, and this is the way it should be. And it's also necessary to have forces of dark-ness and chaos, which creates a dynamo of creation. I think it's something that's beyond good and evil, for sure. I think it offers the opportunity for integrating ourselves into our whole selves and revealing our hidden parts, our shadow parts that are there as well. And I think it's clearly an initia-tion into some kind of otherness, into an acceptance of otherness. Some people stumble upon these experiences, and some people seek them out, but this doesn't happen for everyone. There's a reason that some people experience this. Maybe some are just suited to standing in two worlds.*

◆ ◆ ◆

Elise's closing statement articulates how complex the experience is. The test of mettle combined with the deconstruction of our dualist mindset is a significant challenge, irrespective of your starting position. Actually experiencing these cosmic forces firsthand is deeply humbling and frightening. If your ego is not moderated, it has the potential to reach self-destructive amplification. Nature is unforgiving. It hands out life and death in equal measure. This does not make nature either good or evil. Both light and dark can be consuming. This is something we confront in ourselves when we experience the Dark One. What within me is consuming me? Can I come to an understanding with those destructive elements of myself? Through this initiatory process comes the opportunity to integrate oneself into the whole, to understand one's nature and accept otherness.

9

Jessica Mitchell, Glastonbury Tor

Born and raised in Kansas farm country, Jessica Mitchell encountered a Dark Man on the top of Glastonbury Tor in England in 2011. What occurred that night had a profound effect on Jessica's view of the world.

The depth of mythology surrounding Glastonbury is staggering. From King Arthur to Gwyn to Jesus Christ himself, its legendary associations make Glastonbury the mythological heart of Britain. The Tor rises out of the Somerset levels and is visible for miles. At its summit stands St. Michael's Tower, all that remains of the second St. Michael's church. The Tor has a deep association with Gwyn ap Nudd, the King of the Tylwyth Teg—the Welsh fairies. He is the ruler of the Welsh Otherworld, Annwfn, and his name means Gwyn, son of Nudd. The word *Gwyn* is said to mean "fair, bright, or white," and yet he is described later on as a great warrior with a blackened face. Again we see the now-familiar nondualism metaphor.

In Welsh tradition, Gwyn was known as the "King under the hill." He is associated with certain hills, beneath which he was said to have his palace. Place names like that of the hill-fort of Caer Drewyn near Corwen are thought to have originated from Tref Wyn, "the homestead of Gwyn." Gwyn is also associated with the tradition of the Wild Hunt, which is found in many lands. Given the nature of the Wild Hunt and the gathering of human souls, it should come as no surprise

Fig. 7. St. Michael's Tower on Glastonbury Tor.
Photo by the author

that Gwyn is a psychopomp and is described very clearly as such in *The Black Book of Carmarthen*, one of the oldest surviving texts written in Welsh. Written in the twelfth century, it contains a poem called "The Dialogue of Gwyddno Garanhir and Gwyn ap Nudd" in which Gwyn describes himself as the "hope of armies." In his role as psychopomp he comes from the otherworld to harvest the dead:

> *I have been where the soldiers of Prydain were slain,*
> *From the east to the north;*
> *I am alive, they in their graves.*
> *I have been where the soldiers of Prydain were slain,*
> *From the east to the south;*
> *I am alive, they in death.*[1]

The interview below was recorded for the *Spirit Box* podcast (episode 91). We pick up Jessica's account as she ascends the Tor in the early hours of the morning.

◆ ◆ ◆

Jessica Mitchell

We're mindfully making our way up the hillside and we're looking at the monument at the top. Somehow, we made our way from the bottom of the hill to the top in only twenty minutes, which was baffling to us because we were told that it would take two to three-and-a-half hours to make it to the top. So we weren't quite sure. Knowing what we know now, the three-and-a-half hour timeframe was allotted more for if one was to do the labyrinth to the top, which we weren't, we were just going straight up. So it was a surprise when we were, all of a sudden, at the top and looking at the monument. And by this time it's probably only 4:30 in the morning, so we still have two hours before the sun rises. So that was kind of funny.

But anyway, my friend and I are standing side by side and just taking in the moment, being in the presence of this monument on this hill. There was something really moving about it and awe-inspiring. It was really being in the presence of something ancient. And it's hard to explain just what sort of feelings were stirring inside of me at that moment. But my friend leaned over to me and she said isn't it amazing that it's just the two of us here? And I said yes, it is. It's amazing. And at that very moment I see a small red light appear just to the right of the archway. And immediately my brain says to me, oh, that's some sort of an alarm or a motion detector or something along those lines. But I'm very curious because it appears to be kind of moving around and we're standing about fifty yards from the monument and this red light just kind of seems to be moving around just to the right of the archway. And my brain is trying really hard to figure out what this is. And I asked my friend if she could see this red light and she said no. And right at that moment, the light disappeared and it became this black mass.

I like to explain that it looks like somebody waving a black trash bag. It was blacker than black, and it was angular, growing in size, growing in length and then coming back into being small, and then just being in constant motion. She and I stood there very puzzled by this mass and not really being able to make out what it is. And I tell my friend, you know, I can see it better if I just skew my eyes slightly to the left or to the right. I can make it out a little bit better. But even then, all I'm seeing is this black mass. Nothing taking shape. My friend suggests that we move closer to get a better view of what this is. And I tell her I can't move closer. I can't move, as a matter of fact, because now in front [of it is] . . . the only thing I can describe . . . is a psychic wall that really does not allow me to move past it. So I say I can't get any closer. Right now, I'm frozen in this space. However, I'm going to kind of skirt round this psychic wall. So I move another fifty yards or so away from my friend to get a better side angle of this black mass that's trying to manifest. And she stays where she is, which is head on to the monument and the mass itself. I again move over to a different angle just a short distance away from her. And just as I get to this angle and focus my eyes on what we're looking at, this object begins to take the form of the profile of a man. And I can see him side on. And, like I said, in a profile, he has his back up against the wall of the monument with his leg rested on the wall itself and his arms folded in front of him. And I am in complete and utter shock at what I'm seeing. And about that time, all of a sudden, I feel the energy under my feet begin to move. It feels kind of like ripples under my feet. And I can feel the energy moving from under my feet to this being, drawn in by this being, this black mass, this dark man, as if he is somehow drawing the energy from the ground itself up into his body.

He gathers the energy from the bottom up, and it comes up through him, and the energy comes out of his mouth, and he says, "Good morning," And as he says this, the energy around me is rippling, much like a rock being thrown into the water. And the ripples that come from that, that's exactly what was happening in the atmosphere around us at that time. This greeting of good morning was reverberating throughout the land, is what it felt like, and through our bodies. And I look over at my friend, and she immediately takes this fight or flight stance, as if she's ready to fight. And I start making my way back to her immediately. And as I'm walking back to her, the man comes up off the wall and starts to walk towards us. And my friend says to him, "Oh, my God, you scared us to death," to which he did not respond.

Then he said, "Do you have a cup of tea?" I was so angry at him because I felt violated. My linear brain was trying to make sense of what was happening. Nothing was making any sense to me at the moment, and my reaction was anger. I was extremely angry. But when I heard his voice ask for a cup of tea, something about his accent I recognized. And I wanted to ask him if he was from a certain part of Scotland, because his accent sounded very familiar to me. And it was at that moment lightning struck me and said, "Do not engage"— those words exactly through my mind: "Do not engage." I was given very strict rules not to engage with this being. So I didn't ask where he was from, but his accent did sound very familiar to me.

We said, "No, we do not have a cup of tea." It was puzzling, such an odd question. And then he was visibly disappointed. He said, "Do you have a cigarette?" And again, I was just so angry. And I said, "No, we do not have a cigarette." And again, he was disappointed. And once I made it back to my friend, I said, "How dare you not make your presence known? We've been standing here for five minutes. How dare you not make your presence known?" And I turned to my friend and I said, "We need to go. We need to go now." And so she said to him, "Right, well, have a nice day." And he turns around very slowly. I should also point out he was about as tall as the archway to the monument. If you see a picture of it, it's a big archway. So this being, [this] dark man was well over nine feet tall. He turns around, walks back to his perch on the wall, and gets back into the stance that he was in when we saw him, leaning back up against the wall.

Folded his arms and put his foot back up on the wall. And my friend said, "Well, have a nice day." And he said, "What's left of it," which was an odd thing to say. It's 4.30 in the morning. So my friend and I turn and we're arm in arm, and she said, "Jesse, I think we should run." And I said, "No, we can't run." In my mind, I felt like we were in a very dangerous situation, and if we were to run, it would indicate that we were prey. And I did feel this being was a predator. No, we couldn't run. We could just walk really fast. But part of me really did feel like we were probably never going to be seen again.

We made our way down the hill very quickly, and once we reached the bottom of the hill, we both realized that we were safe. And we spent the next at least twenty-four hours in complete shock and weren't entirely sure what had happened to us, who or what this was that we had encountered, to speak of it. We were visibly shaken to the core by our experience and for the next few days there. But it changed me immediately. I do feel as though I went up the Tor one person, and I came down the Tor after that experience, a totally different person. All of a sudden, everything that I ever thought was true was now turned on its head, and it made me question everything. Something shifted, and to this day, I have been unpacking that experience, and I am learning more and more about it all the time. But it was an incredible experience and one that has shaped me, and I'll never forget it.

Darragh Mason: *Thank you for sharing that, Jessica. What a remarkable and terrifying experience. In terms of the figure that you saw, were there any discernible features? Did he look three-dimensional or just like a flat, dark figure?*

Jessica Mitchell: *Yeah, he looked flat. When I say he was blacker than black, he really was a shade of black that I've never seen in real life. His physical appearance . . . just a profile. The only time that I saw any features was when I was side-on to him and witnessing his profile. And so the features I remember were a very sharp, sharp nose . . . short, cropped hair and kind* *of a pompadourish-type hairstyle. But I don't recall any features other than him being extremely tall. I say he looked kind of like a motorbike rider. He was just all black. But no real decipherable features.*

Darragh Mason: *You mentioned that it changed an awful lot in you. Can you talk about that?*

Jessica Mitchell: *It was a validation to me that these things do exist. It was a validation to me that there was no question anymore as to the existence of other beings, whether they be fairies or ghosts or shadow people. To me, the days of questioning these things were over. Now I knew that this alternate world existed alongside the world that we walk in. I always intuitively knew that these things were real because I had experienced them growing up. I'd seen things, had experiences, but nothing like this. But I always knew intuitively that this was real. But this experience where I actually interacted and exchanged energy with this being, this took it to a whole other level.*

Darragh Mason: *Now, you mentioned that you felt it was a predator. Can you describe what that meant?*

Jessica Mitchell: *Yeah, well, we were in a very vulnerable position, being two Midwestern girls, and (in) a strange land in the middle of the night, and the reaction that I had to that was anger. The predator, he felt like he had been watching us and waiting for us in a way, or waiting for somebody to come up that hill that morning. He just had the air of a predator. It's hard to put into words. I felt like we were in a very dangerous situation, very dangerous. And the way that my body reacted to that situation was to get really angry. And I also knew that just instinctually, that if we were to run, we would probably be killed. But if we were to show strength, we might survive.*

Darragh Mason: *When I've spoken to people who've had similar experiences, where they've seen something just as you described, something that changes their world, that they can't define or that doesn't fit with everything that* *they've, up to that point, understood as being real and tangible, it's quite a shocking moment. It's a frightening moment. It's like you lose your anchor, you become set adrift a bit. What I've found with a lot of people, and I wanted to ask you this question, is when you manage to orient yourself a bit and digest what's happened, you are changed, and your interests and the areas you explore change with that as well. Is that something that's happened to you?*

Jessica Mitchell: *Yeah, absolutely. I feel like I became a little bit obsessed with the image of the Tor, with the monument, with hearing other people's stories about the area. And it did kind of open me up. When I came home from Glastonbury, I started having experiences in my home of seeing entities. There had been some activity in my house already, but something changed where I started having more paranormal experiences. Luckily, that's kind of subsided now. But yeah, there was something about that validation of now knowing that these things exist, and they're real and they're happening alongside us all the time. And I accepted this. I started to see the world in a different light. I started to understand that not everything is as it seems. Yes, I absolutely resonate with what you're saying. And that's how it changed me, helping me understand that there's so much more going on than what we are told or what we see. It's a very complicated and deep place that we live in.*

Darragh Mason: *Have you ever seen him again?*

Jessica Mitchell: *No, I haven't. I've seen another, I've seen a shadow person, but no, not this entity. He's a different energy from your typical, run-of-the-mill shadow person. No, I've not encountered this being again.*

Darragh Mason: *You almost seem disappointed.*

Jessica Mitchell: *I am. There's a part of me that feels as though, after that morning, a piece of him is now inside of me and a piece of me is now inside of him. We exchanged something that day. So even though I was so angry and so scared, there is a part of me that does long to be reunited* *with him, if for no other reason than to just ask questions. "Why" would be the first question I'd like to ask. I've gone back to Glastonbury many times looking for him actually, and never finding him again. But I do hope to meet him again. And now I'll be more prepared.*

◆ ◆ ◆

There are several elements to this encounter that support my belief that Jessica encountered an emanation of the Dark One. The first and most obvious is the Tor's association with Gwyn, which we've explored. There are further, more nuanced elements in both how the dark figure behaved and in the personal aftermath for Jessica. In asking for a cup of tea and later for a cigarette, we see the sense of humor that the Dark Man often exhibits. The requests are absurd and they make light of the extraordinary and traumatic circumstances in which Jessica and her friend find themselves. Jessica describes the figure as having the air of a predator, that should she make the wrong move, her life could be in danger. That if she showed strength, she might survive. This is the "test of mettle," and one Jessica can be proud to have passed.

Finally, there is the personal apocalypse. In her own words, Jessica began to see the world in a different light, that everything is not how it seems. She acknowledges a longing to see him again, a desire to ask questions of him, and that there is now a connection between the two of them. The encounter was an initiation.

10

Shullie H. Porter, Death and the Dark Man

The Dark Man is a psychopomp, and as such has always been associated with death. Hereditary witch Shullie H. Porter was born dead with her umbilical cord around her neck. Her difficult birth gave her the ability to see the dead and the many spirits that exist beyond the veil. Shullie's mother was a Cunning Woman from whom she learned much about the nature of her gifts. In the language of her tradition, "she walks on both sides of the hedge."

What is different in this witness account is *he's* always been with her, and she's always been aware of him in some form. Shullie is honest and frank despite the remarkable subject matter. Her experiences reflect multiple key themes we see within the Dark Man's folklore, from his constant presence on the borders of the otherscape to shape-shifting and the testing of one's character. Furthermore, the hereditary nature of her gifts and practice speak to some aspects of "Fire in the blood." There's been no apocalyptic challenge to her worldview because it was not necessary, and as I've gotten to know Shullie over the last four years, I'm not sure anything can scare her. . . .

◆ ◆ ◆

Shullie H. Porter
___

My mum did magic for everybody. We had a corner shop, everybody came to the shop's back room where she would do magic for people, like getting rid of things. She went to people's houses and laid out the dead; she always went to funerals to make sure even people she didn't know had money to pay the Ferryman.

She talked to the dead, so I grew up with it. My sisters used to see him too, and my youngest sister worked with spirits, as well. She's passed away now, but as she worked with someone too, I really think it might have been him. There have been spirits in all of my houses all my life.

Throughout all the experiences Shullie takes us through, the Dark Man was never far from her or her sisters. With those he follows, he is always there, watching from the shadows.

When I was a little girl, we had quite a large garden with an orchard and chicken sheds. There used to be a man who stood under the little apple tree at the bottom of the garden. I thought he was a policeman because he was tall and dark.

I used to go and talk to this man at the bottom of the garden, a man who wasn't there. Initially, I didn't know that other people couldn't see him. I talked to him for years and years—he was always around throughout my childhood. Recently, I was talking to my sister about it, and she said she remembers the man at the bottom of the garden and that my mum saw him, too. My mum saw lots of things. My sister said she was scared of him, and my mum said to her, "You don't have to go talk if you don't want to." So within the family, it seems everybody saw the man at the bottom of the garden, but I'm the only one that used to go and sit and talk. It took me a long time to realize who that man was because he's been in my life on and off for years.

I've always seen spirits and talked to the dead. I was born dead, I was born with the cord around my neck, a month early, and on the top of the stairs. My mum's next-door neighbor delivered me, she took the cord off my neck and got me breathing. My mum told me that's why

I could see everything—because I was born dead. So I was there and came back. I've died a few times since, and he's been around every time.

In the situations Shullie described, liminality is prevalent. These are places and times of intersection. They are crossroads of both life and geography. The back of the garden is where our living spaces bleed into the natural world. Halfway points between the human world and the wild world. I've had profound experiences of my own in my garden space. I've heard my name called by disembodied voices. I've had my forehead stroked and felt the weight of a hand on my arm when there was not one present. These are shared spaces. They are borderlands with the otherworld. Shullie's difficult birth, along with her hereditary gifts, have given her a constant aperture into a world most of us only get flashes of, like single frames of the pleroma cut into the film of our lives.

He would change shape. When I was a child, he looked like a soldier. I used to show off at school and play with Ouija boards and freak everybody out, and tell their fortunes and do all the magic for boyfriends and girlfriends—all those kinds of things that you do. He was around then, and he used to always be whispering and talking to me. As a teenager, I started to jump trains and go on adventures. My mum died when I was sixteen and after that, I went a bit rogue. I disappeared for a while, but he was always there with me, in the shadows. People talk about shadow people, don't they, and he would be around, like a bit of a shadowy-type thing.

I put him into the back of my mind, trying not to have a lot to do with it, really. I'd got other things going on in my life. I really didn't want dead people talking to me. That's what I thought he was, a dead man.

He really came back into my life in a big way about fifteen years ago, as a definite person, as a definite tall, dark man. I was in a coven; we would call the corners and call things in, and he came forward with lots of other spirits. Now, one of the people in the coven was working with angelic beings, and we thought these spirits were Fallen Angels in some ways, because that's what she was working with. I assumed he was one of them. He used to come and stand with me when this coven did any work, and then go away again. When this coven broke up, he came home with me, and he remained with me, so much so that when I went to places, people would see him. I remember I needed some energy after having done work with lots of people, so I went to the spiritualist church, and he really freaked them out! They said to me and then to my friend, "She's got a big, black man behind her." I knew instantly who it was. I went to America, and a woman tried to read my fortune, and she freaked out, too. She asked if I knew I've got a big black man with me. I said, "Yeah, I know who he is. He's fine." She wasn't happy with him. People have always struggled to read for me too because I think he steps in. Once, I did an Angel workshop, where you go to find your Guardian Angel. There were these women reading for people, giving them their Angels. And telling them they have Michael and Raphael etc., all these "lovely" Angels. She just stopped in front of me and said, "I can't talk to you about yours, because he's big and he's black and he doesn't want me to talk to you." I said, "That's fine. I know who he is. He's not going to hurt anybody. He's looking after my back." I understood by then what he was. I'd try and talk to him but at that time he really wouldn't communicate much with me. I went to Glastonbury, and a friend down there said to me, "I can see the man behind you." This friend, who's into traditional witchcraft, and I started talking about my Man in Black and who she thought he was. I said I didn't think it was Lucifer. He'd never told me his name and I assumed Lucifer would be brighter. It took quite a number of years for him to give me his name. I ended up saying, "If you don't give me a name, I will not work with you. I will not talk to you." So he seemed to give in, and gave me his name.

I've had similar experiences. Psychics have seen him behind me in Witchfather form where he was cloven-hooved and dressed like a seventeenth-century gentry. Another time my father saw him behind

me as a large black figure while I was recounting to him my experiences
with the Dark Man.

*I had to go for some tests in the hospital and have an operation, which
involved going through an artery in my thigh. I had a really bad feeling
about it. I knew I was going to die. I've died before, I've drowned, and
things like that. But this time it felt different, and I really didn't want
to die!*

*I went through the procedure. Nothing happened. I was fine,
I was taken back to the ward, where I had to lay on my back for
three hours. I was not allowed to move or get out of bed. Still nothing
happened, everything seemed fine. Later, my husband and my sister
came to visit me. So I sat up, just a little bit. As I started talking
to them, something went pop, and then I felt the pain. It was like
somebody ripping my thigh apart and the sheet started to turn bright
red. The bed was covered in blood. As that was happening a door
opened to the right of me, and he stepped through. He said, "Come
on," so I went with him. Immediately the pain went away. All these
people that talk about lights and long passages, but that didn't happen
to me, no. I stood in the middle of a desert with him. He said, "If you
want to come with me, we're going to go over there to the abyss." I
wasn't scared and I knew he was going to take me across the abyss.
As we were just about to move on, I looked back, and the door was
still open. Then I could see the tunnel, it was going backwards towards
my husband and my sister, who were standing at the bottom of the
bed. My husband was white and crying, and my sister was screaming,
"Don't you fucking go! You better come back!" I turned back around
to him and said, "I can't come," and went back.*

*As soon as I walked through the door, back into the hospital
room, the pain returned. The door slammed shut and I thought, that's
it. I didn't know if he'll come back again. I didn't feel him for quite
a while, and I was a bit scared of seeing him. Then one day I was
doing a meditation and the door opened again and he's there. I said,*

"I'm not going to die, am I?" He said, "No, you're not going to die, but you can come through." So now I can go through that door every time. I don't have to do a journey, which is what I used to do to get to where I needed to go. I can just open the door. Most of the time I'm still in that big desert, but there are other areas. I know to one side there's a woodland and things like that, and I can go there if I want to. However, most of the time, when I go through, he takes me to this desert, and I can feel the sand under my feet, and I can feel the heat. Occasionally it's nighttime and it's cold, but mainly it seems to be in the day. When we come to what looks like a big abyss, a big gap, there are things going up and down and moving around. I won't say the demonic or anything like that because they don't look like demons as such—they look like Angels, some have wings, some haven't. There are also people moving around. It's like a ladder moving up and down. Sometimes we sit with my feet dangling over the edge and have conversations about life and the universe. And sometimes we just have chats. I can come back quite refreshed.

This has been happening for a few years now, on and off. I now know he's there all the time. Also, since then, my psychic powers have increased. I also work with Hecate. I find when I am working with her, he's there, too. To me, they feel like, I'm not going to say a pair, but that I have them at either side of me. Though Hecate comes and goes, he's a lot more present. Recently I've suffered a number of close family deaths, I mean, five deaths in three years, and I just truly believe he was there throughout all of it because otherwise, I would have absolutely [sighs] . . . . First, it was my father, then my ex-husband, my mother-in-law, my best friend and, finally, my youngest sister. Oh, and my dog, most important, my big black dog. Throughout it, I'd sit and talk to him and walk with him. He gave me a lot of comfort and managed to get me through. Sometimes I crumbled, but he sort of walked with me in that way.

I know who he is now. I don't mind saying his name—it's Samael. The name he gave me is Samael. I work with him, with Samael, but I *don't make deals with him, or I try not to. I keep getting maneuvered into corners where sometimes it's a bit of life and death. He's very tricky, but he makes me laugh and he likes to dance with me.*

The Dark Man is intertwined with death. We see similar characteristics from the Lord of the Dead as we see with the Dark Man. Donn Dubh tricked the Fianna to visit him in his otherworldly fort by sending the Lady Máil to them in the form of a deer. The same magic was used by the Fear Dubh.

Death is the ultimate crossroads, and he is the Lord of the Crossroads. In the traditions around the Wild Hunt, sometimes the Devil leads from the front as the fairy host rides across the night sky accompanied by witches. They hunt for souls seeking out human beings, striking them with their fairy darts. If the darts strike home, the injured party is not long for this world. Death can strike anyone at any time. The question of cruelty and fairness is a red herring. These beings are transmoral and we must resist the urge to project human moralities on them. We must also resist the personification of great spirits like the Dark Man. To do so is to make trouble for yourself. Remember your boundaries and be cunning.

After I had the blood loss, I realized when I went and met him that he was the man that had been with me all my life. He's been around for a long time, so I don't have that kind of fear of him. I've read stuff and thought, should I be scared of this angelic being? Especially when they talk about him being a fallen angel and things like that. I've seen his wings once, and that's when he put his arms around me when my father died. It wasn't scary. They closed around me, it was like a hug. Physically, he's about seven, eight, nine feet tall. Sometimes, when you say a man in black—he's always in black to me—his face can be black but not like a black person. His face is so black it's a void, and you could fall into it and be swallowed up if you're not careful. You can be terrified by it. Or it can be very comfortable. But then, within that void, I sometimes see features. I read something recently about the djinn and about the black djinn, and it just struck me, this may be the same thing, especially as I'm in a desert. Why would I be in a desert of all places?

Darragh Mason: *Has he been around lately?*

Shullie H. Porter: *Yeah, he's around—at the moment, he's always around, though sometimes I have to call him. For example, I recently said, "I need a job, I need some money," and a door opens. Somebody I know approached me and asked if I'd like to go back to something I used to do. Something I said I'd never go back to because it's physically, mentally, and spiritually exhausting. I ended up going back. I think that's his sense of humor: "Well you've asked for a job and as you're not listening to me . . . !" Be careful what you wish for.*

To be fair, I haven't really known what he wants me to do. I do Coffee and Cards and a few of us get the Man in Black all the time. And we joke that it's him saying, get off your ass and do what I ask you to do and believe in it! I think that's the biggest, hardest thing, to believe in it. I've always had to provide for myself. I'm not the most trusting person. Even with spirits, ghosts of the dead, I don't trust them!

Darragh Mason: *So you say he's a comfort, he's a help. Has he been austere with you?*

Shullie H. Porter: *He's told me to pull myself together—sort yourself out—to that effect and, "What are you doing? You've got the abilities!" Like a lot of people, I'm my own worst enemy. One thing he has shown me is that I'm really good at magic, hexing, etc., and creating stuff. I can do dark magic very easily, which I think is from him. The temptation, when someone pisses me off, is not to fall back on that because I can do it easily, that's the negative side of me, which I think he has quite a pleasure in watching. I won't do that; I tell myself I will not be that person. It's like a test. I think that's how you move up, grow, change. I think it was this way with my mother—it's a familial thing.*

◆ ◆ ◆

The matter of hexing and malefica is a challenging one. Malefica is an integral part of witchcraft and one not to be taken lightly, as Shullie describes. It is an intentional act of magical violence. It has its place but should not be employed unjustly or flippantly. When communication has failed and dignified closure of an issue is impossible, or when an imbalance of power doesn't allow for discourse, then quiet punitive action is the witch's justice. As the Christian asks, "What would Jesus do?" others may ask, "What would the Dark Man do? How would the trickster manage this situation?" Nine times out of ten, the answer is indifference.

A witch is sovereign and strives to control their emotions and reactions. They are not led by emotion without observation. A witch is aware of their boundaries and will not allow them to be crossed. If a situation requires one to defend oneself and strike back against an aggressor, then malefica may be appropriate.

11
Megan Rose, PhD

Megan Rose is a transformational psychologist with a PhD in psychology from the California Institute of Integral Studies and an MA in religion from the Graduate Theological Union. The focus of her work is on erotic, occult, and ecological spirituality. She is an initiated Ceremonial Magician, Shakta Tantric, and a Faery Seership practitioner—meaning, she is a witch.

Megan Rose is the author of the book *Spirit Marriage: Intimate Relationships with Otherworldly Beings*. In the book she discusses her own spirit marriage, her awakening to erotic mysticism and her experiences with her fairy beloved, the Welsh deity *Gwyn ap Nudd*. Gwyn is the Dark Man in one of his many forms, and the sexual current that Megan Rose so eloquently describes is recognizable from the testaments of the Scottish witches.

We discuss the current resurgence of the underworld deities. Her viewpoints strengthen my belief that this resurgence is indicative of change, and that we are moving into the time of the witch.

◆ ◆ ◆

Megan Rose, PhD

When we're looking at, for example, the underworld deities, I think there is a kind of emergence-recession-emergence-recession pulsation, where the Old Ones sleep for a while, and then they wake up and rise, maybe take on a new name, shape, or form and begin to shift and change. And I think, in my experience with the Dark Ones (Dark Gods and Goddesses), we're at a point in our collective evolution as a species and planetary epoch that we need a new relationship with the forces that govern our embodiment, our relationship with the body, Earth, women, sexuality—all things that have traditionally been linked to the dark. It's absolutely paramount and vital to where we need to go to survive as a species. After the past few thousand years of patriarchy and its separation of body and mind, we need to reclaim the underworld and its vitalizing energy. When I look at it from a religious studies perspective, I see this rising tide of energy— the reemergence of Earth-centered spiritualities and animism—of which connecting to the dark is paramount. I think that we, Darragh, you and I and a growing number of others, we are in the project of naming, shaping, forming and constellating this new, yet old, form that is coming back—it's never really been gone. One of the things I love about the South Asian traditions is they take their deities out of the temples and they wash them off. Every year there's a time of cleansing and washing of the deities, and I feel like that is what many of us are doing right now with the underworld deities: we're sort of stripping off the past 1,000 years or so of projection and vilification to put ourselves back in right-relationship with them.

I believe the folklore supports this view. An example is the story of Oisín. The Dark Man instigates the events that lead to Oisín's birth. Centuries later, Oisín ends his days in Christian Ireland, mourning the passing of the world of the Fianna. His sad tale represents the decline and disenchantment of Ireland as Christianity moved into the ascendancy. The great hero and poet is a withered old man when he debates St. Patrick, but still he has the tenacity to dismiss the Christian monks as "clerks and bellringers." In Oisín's story we can feel the pulse of the underworld fading. But now the Dark Man current is reemerging; the pulse grows stronger. More and more people are reaching out to me from all walks of life, sharing their experiences with him.

Darragh Mason: *So, about the underworld entities: Who came knocking for you—who did you meet?*

Megan Rose: *I was born with a birth defect, and at less than a year old, I was going to have to go in for surgery. And my mother and aunts and the minister of their church came and anointed my infant body with oil and essentially prayed the Holy Spirit into my body and I was healed. So I was really open spiritually, to the spirit world, at a young age, but in a very embodied, and an often kind of erotic way. And later on in life, after I matured sexually, I would realize that being filled with the Holy Spirit felt a lot like being aroused. And so the other thing that I found really interesting—growing up in the Pentecostal experience—is I would have these powerful ecstatic experiences in church services. But then I would also go out into nature, and I would have that same sort of vitalizing, aroused experience laying against trees, usually singing to them, out in nature. I didn't really see anything wrong with that in my mind, even though looking back I now think, "How very Pagan of me!" But I was never shamed for it—mostly because I wasn't telling anybody about rubbing up against trees!*

I went to seminary and studied religion and spirituality and took this great class on heresy. I became fascinated by alternative forms of spirituality and that was when I was really introduced to witchcraft and to eco-spirituality and to shamanism. That was the mid-to-late 1990s. Then, in the early 2000s, the Dark Ones really came calling after I had a Kundalini awakening experience. I had gone through some devastating and abusive relationships, and had taken up a practice of yoga as one way to heal the trauma and just try and get back in touch with my body. The trauma had sort of shut me down physically, sexually. You see, one of the things that had happened in seminary was I threw the baby out with the bathwater. All of that lovely, embodied spirituality, the filling with the Holy Spirit which I had experienced growing up—I had decided that Christianity was not my path, so I'd shut all of that down. So I was left with this very disembodied, disconnected-from-my-body feeling. Around the time I turned thirty, I started moving into more embodiment-focused practices, as a bodyworker, as a yogic practitioner, and as a dancer. One day, after finishing an asana practice, I was laying in corpse pose, and I felt this vitalism rise up through my body, up through my chakras. And it felt like being filled with the Holy Spirit! But it had absolutely nothing to do with Christianity. So the minute I made that connection between sexuality and spirituality was when the Dark Ones came knocking, because it was almost as if they were waiting for me to reconnect into my physical body so that they could reach through to me. That's when I began to really study Paganism and witchcraft in earnest. And that's also around the same time that the fairy lover started showing up.

Around this time, I realized that I kept getting pulled into relationships for the wrong reasons. And so I thought, "I'm just going to take a sabbatical from dating, take six months and really go deep into my yogic and spiritual practice, and try to understand and heal some of the trauma around my sexuality." So maybe six months after the activation of the chakras laying in corpse pose—I had been doing a six-month celibacy practice—I took a lover. The first moment, I mean the moment that we made love, that he penetrated me, I felt this explosion in my body from my root up to my crown. It was like light bulbs bursting up my spine. Each of the chakras were split open and the energy shot out the top of my head, and I passed out. When I came to, I had no idea what had just happened. Fortunately, I was working with an energy healer at the time, and when I described to her what had happened, she said, "You just had a Kundalini awakening." That was a pivotal moment.

And that energy was nascent inside my body all along, because it wasn't like something came from outside of me, it was like something had awoken inside of me. And it was raw, like a snake unfurling its cobra head. And, you know, what ended up happening shortly thereafter was in my dreams, a spirit lover began to show up. He presented as a kind of powerful, dark, angelic sort of being—what I understood to be fey, and also as this dark man figure.

Sex and sexual energy are mentioned again and again by those who established a relationship with the Dark Man, meaning those who got beyond the horror at his initial appearance and began to work with him in earnest. Isobel Gowdie described sex with him on multiple occasions. He either has direct sexual interest or amplifies the sexual energy within people. Fionn and Sadhbh were overcome with love and desire for each other—perhaps a result of the Dark Man's magic?

And for a long time—ten to fifteen years—we were in negotiations. I was like, "If you come to me, telling me that you're the devil, that you're Lucifer," intellectually I'm gonna understand what all that means, but there's this other part of me that is just going to be like, "No, no, no, I can't go there!" So we need to negotiate and find some other frame that we can use, so I can work with you and not have this internal struggle with all of my Christian programming—which I have committed to dismantling, but it's just going to take me some time. Like, I'll do my work on my end to dismantle this stuff, but, you know, you need to meet me halfway and we need to find a form that my unconscious can get on board with." And so that's really how we arrived at the fairy beloved. It was really a gift when he gave me the name Gwyn. Because in the Welsh tradition, Gwyn is the Lord of the Underworld, or Dead, but also a fairy king, and the Christian tropes really have nothing to say about him. I have Welsh ancestry, and I thought, "Perfect, I can get on board with this."

I'm going to read this fantastic quote from Vivian Crowley. She says, "Most practitioners of Earth traditions do not see their deities as good guys opposed to the universe's baddies. The Divine is neither good nor evil, but a force that permeates the universe. It emerges into action out of eternal tranquillity and contemplation, and returns to stillness once more when each phase of creation is done. There is good and evil, but it is within human beings, not the cosmos. Evil exists not in the form of an external tempter or demon, but in the actions of human beings. The divine itself is neither good nor evil."

The phrase "returns to stillness once more when each phase of creation is done" brings us back to emergence and recession. If we are in a time of emergence, then we are in the foothills of a new phase of creation—one in which all witches and storytellers will play a part.

Megan Rose: *Well, you know there's this idea that light is good and dark is bad, right? But we can have too much light and things fry, then burn out; we end up with a scorched Earth or scorched nervous system. Too much dark, and things seep into complete decay and deterioration. So I go back to my tantric training. Kali gives us the disease, and she takes it away. There's death and destruction, which gives rise to new creation and new life, and we need both. We've been vastly out of balance here in the West, so focused on light and the upperworld, to the point that I think we're experiencing an exhortation from the underworld, like, "You're fucking out of balance, you need to get back in balance." As Jung said, the tree can only grow as high as the roots grow deep. "Y'all need to grow your roots down."*

Darragh Mason: *You refer to Kali a lot, which is interesting. I find that the broad Indian models, particularly Krishna, come up again and again, and there are a lot of similarities between Krishna and the Dark Man.*

Megan Rose: *Oh, that's fascinating. I'm getting chills as you say that because I write about this in my book. I was sitting in a tree and I was meditating and seeing these visuals, and one of the visuals that came was of this blue God. And I was trying to find the name of this being. I had created a sigil, a rose cross name, that I used as a placeholder name for him before he gave me the name Gwyn. I mean I know that fairy people are really reluctant to give you names, but I was like, "Come on, it's been ten years! Can I get a name, please?" And so he was showing me these different faces, and I saw the Peacock God Melek Taûs, and I saw a couple of Dark Gods. And I kept saying, "Well, is this you?" And he would say, "I'm like that, I'm like that": [Reading from her book:] "Before me manifested the Peacock God, a beautiful being with curly dark hair, blue skin and eyes* aflame and all I could say was, 'Lord, welcome, Lord.' And I bowed not out of subservience, but out of honor and respect. And many different associations began running through my mind as I tried to associate this being, this fairy king, with a deity. At first I thought, is it Krishna? And he responded, 'I'm like that, Krishna was based on me.' And I thought, is this Dionysius? And again, he responded, 'I'm like that, he's based on me.' And then I remembered the Peacock God, known as Lucifer from the Anderson Feri tradition. And he responded, 'I'm like that, he's based on me.'"

I think this is the Dark One's M.O. It's not about fixed forms. It's about letting go of the form, letting go of our need to classify in that scientific way. I think that is very much in alignment with the trickster energy, which feeds into this archetype as well. I was just working with one of my clients yesterday, and talking about archetypes and what Jung, I think, really meant when he was describing archetypes. I don't think Jung ever meant for archetypes to be these defanged, declawed, just psychologized things. I mean, if you look at The Red Book, he was working with entities. And I think archetypes were his attempt to really understand the prima materia underneath these different deity forms and forces that arise trans-culturally. One of the things that I really like about Faery Seership work is that the Faery Keys, like the Guardian or the Ancestor, really are archetypal forms and forces. They're not deities—they're not as fixed as a deity—but they are absolutely intelligent and absolutely conscious and interact with us, just apriori to liturgical devotional practices. And that forces us to unmake ourselves to a certain degree to be able to dance with them, hence the traditional warnings about fairy work.

Darragh Mason: *What are your thoughts on generational contact?*

Megan Rose: *One thing he's shown me is that he's been wed to this particular matrilineal line that I carry for generations. And I'm working on reconnecting to that wisdom stream. I did a lot of ancestral healing work at first. When I first started getting in contact with him, I had to do all this heavy lifting of ancestral healing to sort of scrape off the years of abnegation that* *had built up like rust when the women in my line had stopped upholding that relationship. I think these otherworldly forces don't necessarily see us as distinctly as we see ourselves; they see more of the thread of our ancestry or bloodline. We're each like a bead strung along that thread, but they're looking at the thread, not necessarily the individual beads. They don't play by human time-space rules. They're seeing that thread and the continuity of relationship, and if there's been a disruption along the family line, it's our job to go back and remedy the disruption by stepping back into right relationship with them.*

Megan Rose makes a significant point and one which is, perhaps, the key to the mystery of our interactions with him. I have often wondered if the Dark Man perceives us in a similar way to how he presents himself. If his many names and many forms are emanations from the same current—and I believe they are—then it's possible that we are perceived as points on a familial line, not as individuals, but as a whole. That we are an expression of a familial energy in our present time and entangled with our ancestors and our descendants. This is a challenge, not only to our experience of time but to our separation from all within our line. It is building on the challenge to our separation from nature in a very personal and immediate way. If the Dark Man is interacting with the key ancestral and descendant nodes on our familial lines at once, then we have a responsibility to our family lines past, present, and future, one which we must treat with the utmost importance. Our actions have implications for all within our lines, not just to us. We may never see the benefit of that work, but we can take great solace that our descents or ancestors will.

I had a dream in 2015 where I was flying in the air towards Glastonbury Tor, and I landed in this hawthorn tree. I wrapped myself around the hawthorn tree and the hawthorn tree started making love to me. It was after I had that dream that my fairy beloved finally told me his name is Gwyn. And when I shared the dream with Orion

Foxwood, my Faery Seership mentor, he said, "You know that tree exists, right?" But I didn't! Orion said that a sacred hawthorn tree is on the side of Glastonbury Tor and next to it is a large stone that is apparently the testicle of Gwyn in the upperworld, and legend says there's a twin stone, his other testicle, next to it in the underworld. This hawthorn tree is a key access point to Gwyn ap Nudd's fairy realm. So when that name and that specific dream came, it was a pretty powerful confirmation. Then, in 2016, I went on a pilgrimage to visit the Tor, and I had a powerful experience with that tree, which I write about in my book. Later on, in 2018, I found Celtic studies scholar Danu Forest's book on Gwyn Ap Nudd, and all the information in the book was what my fairy beloved had been revealing to me about himself over the years, so it was just confirmation after confirmation of the contact.

The Tor, as we know, is linked to the Dark Man in a tangible way. Yet again we see the folklore map directly to the experience of the individual. I visited the Tor to film a magickal ritual four weeks before I had a spectacular vision of him in angelic form. I cannot say definitively, but there may be a connection. What I do know is that the vision changed everything for me. It was my moment of ontological apocalypse.

Darragh Mason: *A lot of this can be terrifying.*

Megan Rose: *Absolutely, but you know, that's part of the initiatory experience, the terror. You have to go through the deconstruction, the dismemberment, the dissolving. But a lot of folks can't get past the terror. They say, "Oh, no, the Dark Ones are dangerous! No, no, they're scary. Don't go there. There'll be monsters." Well, humans can be dangerous as well, right? We do some pretty monstrous things. But that doesn't mean we reject all of humanity. The Guardian who initially blocks our entry to the underworld and appears terrifying at first, when properly approached, can become the loving Guide who safely navigates us through the otherworldly realms. I think that the Dark Ones unmake us, help us dismantle forms that we* *no longer need, need to compost so to speak, so that we can become more of our True Self. And if you're not prepared, or if you don't respect their potency, yes, it can be shattering. But I also think it's in our depths where we find our power, our magic, our wisdom. So I'm an advocate for developing night vision. Find a transpersonal therapist or a depth coach or a spiritual guide or tradition that can help you navigate the underworld, and then go spelunking!*

12

Orion Foxwood, the Dark Rider and the Crossroads

Orion Foxwood is a witch and Elder in Traditional Craft and is a Southern and Appalachian Conjure man. He is a high priest in Alexandrian Wicca and teacher of Faery Seership and cocreative magic. An author and lecturer, he has given talks extensively across the United States for nearly thirty years, and he has taught and coled magical tours in the United Kingdom.

Born with the veil, he has been steeped in the spirit world since birth; his spiritual heartbeat is composed of the magic and the sacredness of nature. He founded and directs the House of Brigh, which provides a Comprehensive Faery Seership Apprenticeship Program, ancestral healer's training in the "river of blood technique," and training sessions in folkloric-based faery healing and magic practices. He is a teacher of the folk magic, witchcraft, and the second-sight practices and lore of his birth culture in the Shenandoah Valley of Virginia. His practice includes the teachings and methods of his Elders and mentors later in life, and material codeveloped with his spirit-wife, Brigh. He now resides in Maryland.

Orion's understanding of and experiences with both the crossroads spirit and the crossroads magic came first from his folk culture, then later from the witchcraft he learned from his elders and teachers, and from his work in contemporary and folkloric faery practices. He suggests that the *to-the-bone-real* understanding of spirit that lives at the crossroads, and the power of crossroads magic, happen when the lore, teachings, and direct encounter come together as a deep knowing that is the product of experience, over and over. But, like all things, to see is to know about something, but to do is to become wise in the knowing. This is the fruit he offers in this interview.

◆ ◆ ◆

Orion Foxwood

Mostly what I can share with you will be about the Dark Rider, as he was called by my mother and other elders in the Shenandoah Valley, and now by me. I can only tell you what I know and what I know is simple but powerful folk wisdom about a real spirit—one that is feared and revered by the hill folk, the miners, orcharders, farmers and all who live close to the ancient land, the battlefields and often forgotten places, but who still feel him and who still remember how to live right with him.

The Rider lives in the spirit-land, the liminal landscape—along with themfolk (also known as Faery), the grey ladies, devil dogs, hag riders, and a host of other haints known by the old-timers and engaged by the witches, spirit-workers, those born with the veil and the conjurers. These spirits are not simply things we believe in. They are influences that our ancestors knew, unseen neighbors we know now, and kin if you will. They are powerful—uncanny sometimes— and may arrive bidden or unbidden and they have their ways. In short, we don't "believe" in the Dark Rider. We don't believe in "air" either. But, they both are real, and invisible, and dangerous to ignore.

The Dark Rider, in my view, is one of the most ancient and potent spirits I know. He is well known by many names throughout Appalachia and the American South: dark man, devil, papa, and trick-doctor, just to name a few. So, it is my pleasure to speak of him, his ways and powers. Especially at this time when our world sits in the crossroads of change, or in the body of a God; a concept I will explain further in a while. You have to give such information in good order or it won't unfold as it should. I will also share some lore from the faery and the witchcraft lore that I carry, as well as was gifted, researched, or was revealed. In the faery lore I teach, he is known as the Guardian, and in the craft lore he is the Horned One, Ole-Horney, the Dark One/Man etc. In both of these practices, he is horned or antlered, (unlike the Dark Rider who is not). These beings are large in stature, often with hounds, a shadowed face and eyes that glow with power. One horn is the past, one horn is the future, and he often arrives with the two horns crossed. If you bear the mark of the witch or carry witchblood, the two horns open up the hidden way, which is the haunted acre and the gray-road "betwixt and between."

The Dark Rider, however, does not usually come large in stature. He comes sometimes as a dark figure, even like a living shadow. Other times he is a kind grandfather walking with a cane, sometimes singing or whistling. He is called the Dark Rider because he rides a black horse. Let me say a little more about the horned one. He has other ways that he may appear that are, well, less "traditional." I'll give you a couple examples. I was once teaching a workshop in New Orleans at the Folk Magic Festival, an annual event created and hosted by a group of seasoned conjurers, witches and root-workers collectively called "Conjure-Crossroads." I was one of the founders. In the workshop, I presented lore and taught practices that culminated in preparing coins to be taken to a crossroads on their own as an offering to the Rider. One of the attendees—a respected witch and author—took hers to a crossroads in the French Quarter that night. After she performed the work I shared and gave the coins, a dark man in a top hat on a black bicycle rode through the intersection and simply said, "Bless you," as he winded by. This was the Rider in yet another form, and the bike was his horse. In another event where I was teaching in Southern California, we went to the crossroads of an old ghost town. The attendees made their offering of three Mercury head dimes, as we conjure workers call them (the actual name is a "liberty head" dime), and a small cup of Crown Whiskey or rum. As they offered and we knocked on the dark gate (the center of the crossroads), I explained that they may feel or hear something strange, out of place, or disturbing. No sooner had those words escaped my mouth, the characteristic cold breezes came up the four roads and one of the attendees' cell phones went off with the ringtone of a revving motorcycle. There were no phone signals where we were, plus the screen of the phone simply read "unknown"; he did not have that ringtone on his phone and he assured us the phone was turned off long before the workshop. The Rider has many ways of demonstrating his presence. Now, back to the Horned Ones.

Horns and antlers have deeper meanings and powers than most contemporary people understand. In older traditions, they are holy. For instance, the deer in the faery tradition is the psychopomp between the worlds. And this is why often you'll see faery beings riding on deer. The thing about riding on horses, I believe, came a little later. The deer was first. There is an important insight on the sacred presence of the horned or antlered animals in the lives of our ancestors. Their fur and meat often kept us alive in the winter and thus they stood in the fulcrum of life and death during the most life-threatening weather. The horns also pierce the veil between seen and unseen to the thresholds in between. By whatever name he is known, the crossroads spirit is liminal, not human, and he can arrive from the haunted winds, moving from somewhere to here, or from nowhere to everywhere, and these ways of perceiving him can be daunting and terrifying for some, or inspire the delicious shivers in others like you and I.

But the thing is, the Rider always shows up, whether it's with horns that pierce the way or as the trick-doctor that will trick you with the tricks that are in your heart until you see the truth. His arrival is nearly always preceded by howling or barking dogs, silenced night sounds, cold wind, the smell of tobacco, whiskey, animal musk, Hoyt's Cologne, rum, or coffee to name some of his signature scents. He jars you—shakes you up and makes you think hard. You cannot bring any falsity to him whatsoever. In his approach, you feel his piercing gaze penetrating your soul, pushing past niceties, falsities, and anything hidden. He sees what you mean and not what you say. In fact, he knew you before you arrived and his glare sees into your core—where your real petition lies. This is the animating force that gives velocity to intention. It is the true reason you are there at the crossroads, alone, scared, hopeful, humble, and true.

The arrival of the Rider can feel like you are spun around, dizzied, and pierced (and maybe leaking tears or piss), and straddling between uncertainty and assurance, truth and trick, awe and intimidation— between human and other, and you may panic for a moment and even forget where you are and why you came. Have you ever felt that? I think it's good for humans to feel intimidated, humble, and even innocent as a child sometimes. I think it is a good feeling for all people to experience. It fosters humility, awe, and gratitude. I liken it to the feeling I had standing at the edge of the caldera of Mt. Kilauea, the active volcano on the big island of Hawaii. I felt so small, insignificant before such an immense power. Yet, I also felt privileged to be in her presence. For the true witch, our blood boils with power in this "tweeny-state," where one foot is in the human world and the other in the unseen, but felt, spirit world—so immense and all pervasive. This is the reason that witches are seen as not all human.

Now, a little more on my birth culture and earliest relationship with what I know as the Dark Rider. I come from the Shenandoah Valley, where the Blue Ridge Mountains go down into the valley, right where at the western tip Appalachia is pouring into deep Southern Virginia culture, so you get this real mix of stuff aggregated where a deep valley and ancient mountains meet. Appalachian culture pours down from the mountains with Celtic, German, Scottish and Irish elements and mixes with Virginia Southern culture which has

English folk elements and the strong influence of Africa through the trans-Atlantic slave trade. I honor the Ancestor of all of these roots, especially considering the horrors of slavery and respect to the source of many of the components of my conjure.

My Momma was born in a slave quarters on a plantation on January 2, 1934. Interestingly, her birth digits come out as 1/2/34. The midwife or "Granny Woman" as hill folk would call her, was a freed slave. Her and her mother were emancipated when she was like five or so years old. Miss Granny was the person who told my Momma about the Dark Rider. Momma considered her to be a saint. When she visited, all of us kids had to be clean, well-groomed, and on our best behavior. Neither she nor Momma called themselves anything. They considered themselves to be Christian, but it was what some anthropologists call "folk Christianity." I could never tell them they were conjure workers or witches. They just knew things that you do to get what you need. So, here's a little of that knowledge that I share with you with respect to my ancestors and the many workers before me who walk with me: those seen, unseen, and thresholds in between.

The Dark Rider has a time when you seek him. However, he can seek you anytime and anywhere if he has such a calling. Before you go to him, you have to get your spirit right. You have to take a bath with vinegar, coffee, a tiny bit of ammonia, or your urine and lemon juice. Either use a clean white towel to pat yourself dry or just air dry. I also recommend that you crown—anoint—yourself with hyssop oil or tea. If you can wear red, white, and black on you, that would be good. He likes it when you get yourself right for him. Go to him at three in the morning on Wednesday. Three is the witching hour. Three in the morning is the time when I always say both light and darkness loosen their grip and give way to shadow, and you're caught between the heartbeats of creation, and caught between its breaths. Wednesday, three in the morning: that's the time to wake up, sink into the fire of desire, nestled in your most authentic self, and traverse the haunted way to a force older than you can imagine that knows you better than you know yourself. By the way, you can arrive at three or leave for the crossroads at three, but aim to be done by 4 or 4:30 a.m. He falls back into the horizon as the sun rises.

The explanation of why the deer is so symbolically important in Orion's tradition is illuminating. We find again and again the deer provides a suitable intermediary form for the Devil and fairies to embody. Isobel Gowdie described copulating with the Dark Man while he was in the form of a deer. From the *Sorcerer* of Trois-Frères cave to Baphomet, the horned spirits have walked alongside us since the beginning.

Now there's a mystery about the crossroads that a lot of people don't know, and this is very much in the oral tradition: that it's not just any old crossroads. You got to go to the old crossroads. The old crossroads are colonial. And the colonial crossroads were often built on Native American trade routes. Native American trade routes follow animal migration patterns, which follow the magnetic leys of the earth. These are the spirit roads, faery trods, and power beds that flow with the liquid light of the stars in the land and they have power that is real and powerful. At these places we can feel how power falls from the stars into the earth, then rises up and out to the horizon and back in again. Working these trods are one of the hidden secrets of this work.

When those leys cross each other, they form a "well of power" at the center. That's the power-point where magnetic and electric streams of power give and take, where the worlds breathe, and it is the mercurial movement of this that is the horse upon which the rider comes. It is where everything thins, nothing claims or confines but moves in serpentine undulation in and out of nothingness. If you can't get to one of those, you go to a bridge over water, and that's the most potent crossroads of them all because it cannot be claimed by heaven, hell, or the land. It's betwixt, and the most powerful place is right where the bridge crosses water, because you're in the air, off the earth, over water. Barring those, track paths in the woods where animals migrate is excellent as well.

And the way I was taught is, when you do it there, you're in the body of the dark rider. Every time that you've ever been at a crossroads in your life—an intersection where choices are made—you're sitting in the body of a god. People will say, "I'm at a crossroads in my life right now," and what they really mean is they're at a place of ambivalence: "I see the future changed; I see the past that's either resolved or not resolved, and I see or don't see the options before me, but I know that I must change. I've been summoned by divine directive, divine discontent, or ancestral paradox. I've been summoned there." And at that moment, you're sitting in the body of the threshold lord. Now, too often folks think that the beings are only geo-located, and I say that each dark rider at each crossroads is a cell of the body of the greater one. And we are cells in the body of greater things—like everything is—and so, whenever you're caught in that place that we would typically call the crossroads, stop and lower yourself into the presence of the Dark One and you will feel him stronger there than ever. You can make offerings in that moment. And that's what people don't realize. When I'm at that place, I feel it, I feel a mixture of fear, confusion, excitement, and I don't care where I'm at, I get down and I knock on the floor three times. And Dark Rider opens the way. And then I spin counterclockwise three times, so I'm spinning away from the world of man into the world of the spirit. And right then, right there, I'll make an offering. Because the crossroads can also be anywhere: past, present, and future, all suddenly intersecting, giving and taking.

The physical crossroads are where we're tapping geomantic energy. You definitely feel geomantic energy in the faery practices where faery kings are threshold powers and guardians of the entry into the under-country. The fairy queens are colonial, but not like human colonial, they're the aggregate spirit of the place, the entire network of the ecosystem or understrata, for instance, of that place. The kings are the threshold that opens and closes. The mysteries of the whole

and the mysteries of the part. But when I go to the crossroads, I do
the stuff that I grew up with. And Momma told me about him. My
grandma told me about him. But of course, Grandma said, "He's the
devil. You stay away from there!" And of course, that really means
there's power there. Keep your hands out of that cookie jar!

The events that drive the key stories of the Fenian Cycle forward
take place in the wild. Deer and boar presumably travel or are hunted
along similar migratory paths to the ones that formed the crossroads
of America. The wild world reacts to their presence. Fionn crosses a
boundary, and his fate is transformed in the process. Wildness returns
with them to the human world and the story is driven forward. It is
within the walls of Fionn's fort that Sadhbh takes a beautiful human
form, and they become lovers. It is outside the boundaries of his fort
that she is transformed back into a deer, a more suitable form for this
intelligence, a faster form, more suited to the forests and the mountains
than the upright bipedal form.

The *Sorcerer's* composite body reminds us the devil can navigate all
worlds. His body is betwixt and between, just as the Trois-Frères cave is
between us and the otherworld.

Where I come from, there's often other spirits on the way to haunted
crossroads where he is—you may run into Gray Ladies and then you
have to be careful. The Gray Ladies show up as these old women
walking the road, and they'll often show up late at night. If you see
them, you do not stop. And whatever you do, you don't let them
touch you because if you do, you're dead. We have a lot of stories
about them and I've seen them many a time on the way to the
crossroads. So if you walk to the crossroads, you may see them.
Another interesting spirit you may encounter is "Jesus on the road,"
or as a friend calls him, "hitchhiker Jesus." I kid you not, "Jesus on
the road"! And I had it happen once, but a lot of workers say they've
had it many times where they're walking and they're carrying their

heart with them, ready to bear it at the crossroads, and then all of a sudden they'll feel what feels like an angelic host beside them or something. A lot of the old preachers are what we call two-headed preachers. Two-headed preachers work in a pulpit by day and as a conjurer worker by night. Sometimes you'll feel these walking with you. I heard it. I remember once he said, "What seek you, my son?" And I was a little humbled as I was still a little bit more steeped in folk Christianity, which is what I grew up with, which is very different from regular Christianity. I remember just going, "Jesus, is that you?" And it just goes, "If that's what you call me." And all it does is advise you as you're walking, make sure that your heart is clean. I don't know if he comes to everybody, but my elders call him Jesus by the road or Jesus walking the road. If you're going to the crossroads, the encounter with Him has already begun. As I say this, I can feel the ancestors so strongly, because you never walk alone. As you're walking to the crossroads, all those who have ever walked it are walking with you in some way. All those in your blood who know this way are walking with you. And I was always taught that the power gathers on the way there. The magic doesn't begin at the crossroads: it began with the calling to the crossroads. In many ways, the body of who he is is gathering on the way there. That's why a lot of workers will say, "Get yourself clean, get your heart clear before you go there." Because he can also be a mirror that will reflect back to you the content of your heart.

First time I went, I got my tail whooped, too, because I was like seven years old. No, I was older than that. It's closer to ten, I think. So I was told, do not go, never go, because I asked Momma about it. I was really facetious, and Miss Granny had told me about it. I was wanting to go. And so Momma said no, absolutely not. She said, "No, you're not old enough! You stay away from the devil. Go to church!" And I went to the devil. I snuck out. I went and got cookies to take. What does a little kid take, right? And the truth is, to the dark rider, that was gold, pure gold, because it was sincere. And I knew just the crossroads I was going to. It was a little walk, but it was enough that a little boy really shouldn't be out there that late at night. I'm scared as fuck all the way there, right? So I get there and I'm looking around and I swear I can still feel that feeling, even as I talk to you, it was like the whole world went silent. It was like everything was waiting.

I knew about the knock, so I knocked and said, "Mr. Dark Rider, don't hurt me, but I really want to see you. Don't be scary." There were owls around and I heard other sounds, sweet-sounding birds and cicadas and crickets and all these beautiful night sounds. And then the fireflies started up like crazy. And so in retrospect, I think he changed things for this courageous little boy. And I got down, real humble because that's what Miss Granny said. She said, "You got to be real humble. You can't go there thinking you're going to tell them anything. You can't go there hiding anything." She said, "Just lay out your heart. And if you do, you'll get the brightest angel in heaven." That's what they refer to Lucifer as: the brightest angel in heaven. So I got down and I knocked, and I had all the offerings ready and my three Mercury head dimes. Are you familiar with those? I think they're really called liberty heads. Try to get a leap year one, they're the lucky ones. And you carve a little hole through and then put a thread through, and you wear it on the ankle of the foot you step out of bed on. It's really powerful. And if you wear that to the crossroads, you'll never be harmed.

So I knocked and I heard him coming, on a black horse. In our tradition, he comes on a black horse. Usually you can't see his face, and he's a very imposing man. And it's hard to make out what he's wearing a lot of times, but it looks like he has a coat or a cloak, but it goes back into the night itself. It's made of the fabric of the night. I knocked. In the practice I grew up with, knock connects. I sang, "Knock on the dark one's door. All things are as they were before. By earth, water, wind and flame, bring magic up in the old one's name." And so I got down and I knocked and did the spinning three times around and then I heard it. First the wind rushed up from the four quarters, and it was chilling. And then the hounds from everywhere! I don't even know where all these dogs were, but you heard them howling like crazy. It was in a hollow, so it was echoing. So by then I'm almost ready to pee my pants! And I could hear breathing. And then, you know how you hear a horse on top of the ground? I heard it rising from under the ground. Wow! It took everything for a little boy to hold on, to stay there. And then everything went still and what did I really see? I never saw him fully, but I remember a hand touching my shoulder and it felt like all my fear just went away. I felt the hand. I didn't want to look. If you've ever been to a doctor that's got bedside manner, which is rare anymore, they are powerful. They have the ability to just touch you and look in your eyes and suddenly you just know you're going to be well. They're really amazing. And so that's what it felt like. And I heard clear as a bell, "My son, what's a little boy doing at the crossroads so late at night?" And when I tried to explain years later to my Momma what I heard, I said, "It was like hearing Dad's voice, Granddad's voice, the voice of my Uncle Charles all at the same time." That's what was interesting because I could hear the tones and even my brother . . . I could hear the tones of every man in my life who I loved and who I felt the strength of. So he became what I needed. Certainly, my heart wasn't false, so he became what I needed. And all I did was ask—because there was a lot of domestic violence and stuff in the family and we were Appalachian— "I'm so afraid of my folks hurting each other and please, soften their hearts, please!" I think back: it was so sweet, and you know, where I grew up at night in the summer, there are sounds and smells that are incredible. And one of them is honeysuckle. All of a sudden, I swear there was the sweetest honeysuckle smell in the air. And—I'm almost crying now thinking about it—what I felt was the kindest touch on my heart I think I've ever felt in my life. Because I think what he did was not only help with the family, he was also lifting sorrow off my heart. My experience with the Dark Rider is he can humble you, but he can also lift you up. And it's all based on what the content of your heart is when you go. We're assembling his body as we arrive! I have found everything with him is about choice, in that we get the content of our heart. And still to this day, when I work at the crossroads, you know, when it's that time when you're like, okay, it's done, it's done, suddenly you feel him receding away.

Orion's account of meeting the Dark Rider is truly profound. His description of his voice is exactly as I experienced. It was like the voice of every man important to me overlaid at once. I recognized it, yet it was new. There was no discernible accent. Its timbre was clear and rich. It wasn't experienced as an external sound coming from elsewhere. It is experienced within.

Sometimes he comes in strange ways. And when you're working in old magical traditions—we're talking old animistic stuff—we don't look at things as symbols. We look at things as just what they are, right? Like, you go to the Dark Queen of the Underworld and she gives you an apple. Don't go, "Oh, it must be wisdom." It's an apple! You can't always go on the symbolic thing: that's very humanocentric. These are living, powerful, ancient beings. They come as they come. Or to quote this Christian minister out in Tampa, I was there and I was going to be speaking at his church, and he said his elder told him, "Who am I to tell God how to walk into the room?" That's one of the wisest things I've ever heard. We lean on this humanocentrism a little too much and we need to have experiences that make our knees wobble. Shake us a little bit. And make us see that there are powers more ancient and greater than us and we're just lucky that they care for us.

Sometimes the elders would tell frightening stories of the crossroads. Frightening to keep the curious away, to protect the crossroads and those who go there because it reduces the number of folks who go and keeps it safe. And, also remember that a lot of these practices come from a time when you could get arrested for being a witch or any number of things. With the crossroads in America—I don't know if it's still this way or not—but during the colonial times and the Reformation period, at least into the early 1900s, a crossroads was not owned by anyone. It could not be opened because it had to be accessible to everyone, which meant it was betwixt and between.

13

Peter Grey and
Alkistis Dimech

Peter Grey and Alkistis Dimech are the founders of Scarlet Imprint, a leading independent press that publishes works on magic, esotericism, and the occult.

Peter is the author of *The Red Goddess* (2007), which has inspired a renewed interest in the goddess Babalon. His *Apocalyptic Witchcraft* (2013) has been quite rightly called the most important modern book on witchcraft, placing it in the mythopoetic context of the sabbat and in a landscape suffering ecological collapse. His *Lucifer: Princeps* (2015) is a study of the origins of Lucifer. His collected writings, along with those of Alkistis, are published in *The Brazen Vessel* (2019). His most recent work is *The Two Antichrists* (2021), on the Antichrist workings of Jack Parsons.

Alkistis is an artist, dancer-choreographer, and writer exploring the occulted dimensions of the carnal body and its subtle anatomy. Her art and praxis are grounded in *ankoku butô*, a form of Japanese dance theater, which she has practiced since 2002. She has performed solo and in collaboration with musicians and artists in the United Kingdom, Europe, and the United States. She has also spoken on her practice and led workshops at conferences and events on both continents.

In this interview we discuss the primal experiences resulting from encounters with the Dark Man. These primal experiences can lead to a tension with participation in modern digital platforms and highlight the need for us to protect our imaginal spaces.

◆ ◆ ◆

Darragh Mason: *One of the significant things that I found when I was putting this together was this idea of the dark womb, a pool of water within a cave, which kept coming up. And I looked into some of the therianthropic figures within cave art and went straight to the figure of the* Sorcerer, *and then I read* Apocalyptic Witchcraft, *and you discuss the same art. In Isobel Gowdie's confession, she describes him coming in the shape of a deer or a dog. My interpretation of that is it's presenting this kind of non-dualistic reality, representing all aspects of nature. And then the other metaphor is the Dark Man—the illuminator, the light within the dark, and the dark within the light. It's constantly putting forth these different metaphors.*

Then I read your piece, and two days later I'm in the British Museum and there's a book about folkloric monsters and I open it and it's exactly on the page of the Sorcerer. *I got those kinds of prompts, and they're bang on target. I hadn't really had any intention of talking about therianthropic figures, but I was led that way. So I wanted to ask you about how this current presents itself.*

Peter Grey: *Yes, I think it's always going to be a lot of preverbal, unlettered material that characterizes the current. When we were talking and working around* Apocalyptic Witchcraft, *we also went back and were reading a lot of the anthropological material, going right back to the cave and looking at those figures. One of the reasons I went in this direction with* Apocalyptic Witchcraft *is because I was so unimpressed with the direction neopaganism had gone in. It seemed to have lost that sense of primal experience, of this first experience that you're talking about that I think is common to witchcraft. It is that unnerving aspect of it; that non-human, unfiltered encounter which I think takes us back inevitably to the cave. The cave is where you end up looking at primal places of terror.*

Alkistis Dimech: *I had an experience in the woods, a remote forest in northern Greece, and it was a full moon. A strange kind of unnatural terror and* *the blood-chilling feeling of a presence watching me. And I think it's this encounter with something, which is beyond any understanding or any ability to even put into words, that's what you're grappling with. It takes on so many forms, precisely because it can't be pinned down, it has that same protean quality as nightmares. It is so full of this power that it assumes many forms. It inhabits and seizes your imaginal, which is how it seems to work. I think that's one of the reasons that this figure of the Dark Man, as you call him, is such a protean and theriomorphic figure.*

Darragh Mason: *And I certainly have had that feeling of terror. I think that seems to be part of it, almost like a part of the formula of the experience. It's the trial. You've got to get through that before you get to something deeper or something that's meaningful. But we're using language to try and pin down the intelligence of something that's beyond language, and that's a real struggle.*

It took me a long time to get comfortable with what was happening. It culminated in a ritual with two of my witch colleagues down in Dartmoor, where we went out to the moor and we called him. It was terrifying. Communications kept coming through in meditation and these essentially pushed me towards focusing on this book. Prior to that, the communications explicitly directed me off social media, which presents challenges as I have a podcast to promote. But I got the direct communication: to shut it down and don't engage with it.

Peter Grey: *Yes, I mean, there's a profound conflict between this and the neopagan experience. If you attend a ritual and everyone's like, "welcome home, you're back," and, "these are your people," that is very different to the experience that you're talking about, which is the experience of the contact with the Other, which has this extremely deep-rooted fear response in the middle of it. It's a complicated and challenging space to try and find yourself in, and it's one that's very difficult to create in a nonnatural setting. It's hard to produce that effect on people. If you're doing a ritual in someone's front room, you're not going to get that same ingress, the sense that your place in the food chain has been significantly changed.*

Alkistis Dimech: *The forces that you're surrounded by are not something you've devised.*

Peter Grey: *Yes. You've gone out and met it.*

Alkistis Dimech: *I'm really intrigued that this strong feeling came through for you in communication with this intelligence, because both of us and Scarlet Imprint are pretty much off social media, except for a very small aperture. There was a similar imperative behind that as well, the sense that whilst there's a necessity to keep a certain amount open, doing this work doesn't permit you to be visible in the way that a lot of what passes for esotericism or occultism is now. And this practice is so at odds with what's going on in the public sphere, the social media sphere, that it's very intriguing that you had the same reaction. It's making me think about the imperative to be away from social media. The part of your consciousness that is being filled and inhabited with this voice, this song, is in conflict with that. The superficiality, the distraction, is completely inimical to that deep, deep well of consciousness that you actually need to be drinking from. The chapter on dreaming in* Apocalyptic Witchcraft *is pointing to that. We need to take back our imaginal space and actively work with it and fill it with riches and free ourselves of the incessant noise. I find it really tiring to spend time on screens, and social media is the most compulsive vector of that. There's too much information and it fractures consciousness into incoherence. And I think what's needed for this kind of deep spirit work, particularly with a voice that's prehuman— that contains many dead voices within it, and not just of humans, but of animals—I think you need to be able to go very deep, and you need to be very coherent in order to hear that voice and to engage with it. Turning away from social media in order to do this work is the only way it can be done.*

Darragh Mason: *I think that's beautifully put. And I found, reading* Apocalyptic Witchcraft *now, almost eight or nine years after it was written, we live in a kind of very different world, like we have the total proliferation of devices. Technology fundamentally dominates our life with such penetration that we barely have a concept of really how utterly absorbed into tech-*

nology we are—to the point where it is changing our bodies. And when we spoke last, Alkistis, you mentioned Peter talking about people having office bodies—that kind of hunched-over-the-keyboard look. That there is a physical devolution of sorts, or deterioration, and there's all the kind of the health stuff—we've talked about blue light and all that kind of stuff. But fundamentally, contact with this intelligence is through the natural world. And you've got to be out there to experience it. I see some people on social, who clearly live in that digital space, and are totally immersed in it, and I genuinely ponder how they can have a spiritual existence. I'm honestly not judging. I just don't understand it.

Peter Grey: *I don't think people in the digital space can tell the difference. I don't think they're deliberately being deceptive. I just think that they genuinely are not aware of what's missing. I think we've run the experiment long enough now to see whether the digital media interface was going to make people into better magicians or not, and it hasn't. It clearly hasn't. It's made people worse, it's divided people more, it's fractured their attention, and it's shifted the reason for why they do things to the quest for social capital, which is hugely problematic. Witchcraft thrives in the dark.*

There is no doubt that parts of this discussion will upset people who feel we are being critical. I ask those individuals to really examine why they may feel that way. What is causing that reaction? This requires honest reflection on one's relationship with digital spaces. If social media is one's job or is necessary for one's income, then the platforms are working for you, facilitating necessary aspects of your life. If this isn't the case, you're handing over your time, your most precious resource so billionaires can monetize your data. This isn't news. Quite simply, engaging with this work is immensely benefited by proximity to nature, be that a city park or a mountain side. Total immersion in a social media space does not. That is my experience. Just like visiting the beach is easier when you live on the coast—it's not impossible to get to from an inland city, but it's harder and less likely.

Wild spaces demand you listen, they demand you observe. Nature pulls you to engage all senses purposefully. Social media immersion hooks you into a somnambulist cycle of performative and unconscious reactions. Limiting your time in digital spaces to focus on what benefits you is a tremendous act of self-care.

Darragh Mason: *In terms of nature, within this work I'm at pains to be clear that it's nature asking you to withdraw into it, and as it does so it reveals a face to you that is a visceral face, it's fangs and claws and the joys of fecundity as well. It's all of those things intertwined, and you can see that and how the Dark Man behaves with the Scottish witches.*

Peter Grey: *There's that element of cruelty that's in it, which is simply the face of nature. And it's very difficult for moderns to appreciate that aspect of it. It's like taking a pain pill—the second that one feels that any aspect of their body exists, they are immediately reaching for their synthetic opiates. People aren't used to being in any kind of discomfort. They're not equipped for it.*

Alkistis Dimech: *I think people are in a state of inflammation, almost permanently, as if they're waiting to be outraged. The readiness to take offence at perceived slights, or any deviation from a narrow orthodoxy. It's a hyper-reactive state, and that's a product of modern life, the need to present online, not existing if you don't, that's part of what's unhinging people's nervous systems. And they're taking drugs, whether it's highly sugared coffee or denatured foods, to try to soothe or silence the body, which is breaking up under stress and continual assaults.*

Peter Grey: *But again, this is witchcraft. It's not for everybody. In any culture, you're going to find the majority of people are necessarily householders, and there's nothing wrong with that.*

Alkistis Dimech: *But more and more I see that very few people are capable of that experience . . . to bear that. You don't get thanked for telling the truth, do you? All these ideologies are swimming around now, tak-*

ing hold of people's consciousness. I don't think a lot of people have the witchcraft experience you're talking about. They don't have that encounter experience. Ideologies grab them. Spirits don't communicate in those terms—it is darker, oblique, and ambiguous. The wild experience— whether it's being seized by a goddess like Babalon, or whether you've gone out onto the moor at night and you're invoking the dark man— this is something which is beyond any kind of ideological structure, it's beyond even language. It's totally alien and it's totally direct; you feel that in your body. There's no mistaking it. These are just such remote experiences to people now.

Peter Grey: *I think as a result, one of the things that happens when you're working with these kinds of forces is that you will be "othered" for doing it. Partly there's an othering of oneself. One steps away from certain things. The reaction to doing this kind of work and having the imprint of this kind of entity experience around you will mean that people don't rush up to you! It will create a degree of necessary distance.*

Alkistis Dimech: *It puts you in the midst of some chaotic energies.*

Peter Grey: *When you bring this experience out to people indiscriminately, they will react badly to it. You can't give this experience to people who aren't equipped for it. You suddenly discover how much power there still is contained in these things.*

◆ ◆ ◆

I find Peter and Alkistis's honesty in these matters both refreshing and important. Their words resonated with me long after we spoke, not least because the conversation was an opportunity for me to share my thoughts with people I respect, who have a deep understanding of this territory. This conversation shows how the Dark Man experience pushes us to protect our imaginal spaces, to maintain their integrity from the encroachment of invasive technologies and their wake.

The witch has always been othered and always will be. That is why they separated themselves from communities, living on the peripheries of human society. It should be no surprise that the same impulse is present in the digital age. It is simply the nature of the traditional witches' vocation, a primal experience in the realist sense. One that takes us back to the cave.

14

David Beth on Master Leonard

David Beth was born and raised in Africa and lived all over the world in service of the mysteries. He was initiated as a priest of Haitian Vodou (Houngan Asogwe) in Port au Prince, Haiti, and is the presiding Heresiarch of the Leonard Society, a witchcraft devoted to tellurian and chthonic mysteries operating within the meta-current of the Kosmic Gnosis. David is also the cofounder of esoteric press Theion Publishing and has lectured and published his writings internationally. In this interview, David offers us his insight into the deeper nature of the entity known as Master Leonard, who is also known as *le Grand Negre* or the Black Man.

◆ ◆ ◆

Darragh Mason: *Can you outline how Master Leonard (ML) relates to traditional witchcraft?*

David Beth: *While the Leonard Society has indeed been called a witchcraft, their members usually reject this label as too narrowing and restrictive. The Leonardian witches of the Leonard Society prefer to call themselves the Night Watch or Night Guardians. We are of course aware of important folkloric transmissions of the Black Man, such as his associations with corn and corn demons in the German speaking territories, his central role in the records of the witch trials, and Leonard's appearance in certain*

Fig. 8. Illustration of Master Leonard by Louis Le Breton
in the *Dictionnaire Infernal* by Jacques Collin de Plancy,
6th edition, 1863.
Wikimedia Commons

works of demonology and so forth. While we take note of these sources and may find within them fragments relating to the deeper nature of the Black Man or Master Leonard, such information is only peripheral to the Society's experience of this daemon. Since our work is entirely unique in scope and focus and can hardly be grouped together with most of what passes as traditional witchcraft or witchcraft in general, I can only speak of Leonard as they* relate to our Gnosis alone.

Darragh Mason: *Please do elaborate the role of Master Leonard in the work of your Society.*

---

*Despite his name, Leonard must not be thought of as male. As a kosmic demonic force, (s)he partakes of both male and female essences.

David Beth: *Leonard may be best understood in terms of an egregorial entity—if we take an egregore not to be an artificial thought-form created and sustained by a group of initiates but as an enthusing daemonic power which, at some point, was drawn to and made contact with a circle of gnostico-magical practitioners involved in a biocentric form of esoteric work. A pact was forged and Leonard became the mystical guard and focus of the Society, guiding its initiates in their gnostic and magical development. The current leader of the Leonard Society, the Heresiarch, is in charge of feeding the spirit at regular intervals in order to sustain its power in special ways. However, all members of the Society are initiated into the presence of Leonard and may connect with him—in fact, it is the eroto-magical exchange between Leonard and the individual members of the society, his pouring himself out into the souls of the initiates, which rejuvenates his presence as an enthusing daemonic image. The initiates, pregnant with his inseminations, gaze upon primordial images through what has been termed* esoteric vision *or* night-consciousness, *an experience which triggers magical births in word, gesture, and deed. In order to understand the role of Leonard, or the Black Man, in our "sabbatic" work, we must briefly summarize some central principles of the Kosmic Gnosis, the esoteric current within which the Leonard Society operates:*

> The Kosmic Gnosis recognizes a cosmic struggle between opposing forces, the Soul and the Spirit (or logos, pneuma, nous), and their connected biocentric or logocentric worldviews and experiences. The biocentric experience was expressed in chthonic religions of the homo religiosus. Born from androgynous Chaos cum maternal Urgrund, the Kosmos was polarized into body and soul. Every phenomenal appearance was the expression of a soul, and every soul was revealed by a living body. The world pulsed rhythmically in ceaseless mating, the enthusing forces interpenetrating each other and weaving Kosmos at every moment. Prehistoric humankind, in what our Gnosis calls its daemonic stage, developed the faculty of vision, which is not

so much related to eyesight alone as to a holistic experience of the collective senses which allows the Kosmic interplay to come to visionary appearance. This visionary ability was not a faculty of "spirit" or rational consciousness but an integral ability of the soul to receive the images of the world and gaze at their reflections, leading to the most comprehensive experience and engagement with the All. Chthonic religion, as we understand it, is the natural response to the visionary experience of the images or daemonic powers and provides the foundation of true cultus and magic. Tales of a Golden Age, the paradisical rule of Saturn or the time of the Titans, all seem to reflect memories of the ancients of a period in which such daemonic consciousness dominated the experience of humankind, where the individual was not a finite person threatened by death as the end of the self but an embodiment of a daemonic force, which death would transform but not end. The experience of cyclical time ensured that nothing was ever lost and would come again in ever new form. Life was only possible at the cost of death, but Life also encompasses death as its necessary cradle and, in fact, major source of empowerment.

At the dawn of history, a parasitical force emerged within humanity's metaphysical organism: Ludwig Klages calls it the spirit. Alien to the natural polarity of body and soul, it splits body from soul and soul from body and leads to a gradual alienation from the daemonic reality of the world. By manipulating and deconstructing the soul-based ability of visioning the spirit triggered the development of the self-consciousness of the rational "I." Humanity stepped into history or historical time when day-consciousness supplanted the night-consciousness of the daemonic human. No longer was man able to experience the qualities of the world through holistic engagements with their forces, but now operated in the All as an exile, determining his place in the world by what he can rationally understand through analysis and detachment. The spirit expresses itself through the self-conscious "I," creating an individual that fights against the flow of time and struggles to maintain its identity against the dark, daemonic forces which attempt to compromise or obliterate his rational self-awareness. The ancient, complementary daemonic forces or living images that were beyond good and evil had to give way to new Gods, such as the Greco-Roman Olympians, reflecting the projected rational identity and self-awareness. The reductionism and deconstruction of the living Kosmos led to an inability of humanity to connect meaningfully to the enthusing forces, and the sacrality of the maternal daemonic Kosmos was degraded in favor of a world of abstract ideas and deities mirroring this idealism and transcendence. The revolt against the daemonic Kosmos is reflected in the battle and subsequent defeat of the Titans by the Olympian Gods. Apollo the Python killer, Herakles, the man of deeds and merciless destroyer of all the creatures of the maternal world, are mythic symbols of the emerging new world of the spirit: a hierarchical cosmos, structured according to ideal divine laws and rules. While certain marginalized currents of ancient spirituality still retained remnants of the maternal daemonic Kosmos, amongst the most prominent of course being the Dionysian cults, it was the Abrahamic religions that struck at the heart of the tellurian world. They denied and demonized the divine images and established the transcendental paternal One God as the creator of the All, ex nihilo. Through the agency of the Abrahamic prophets, the Spirit managed to create its own hollow idol, the monotheistic God-Image, which leads humanity even further astray from the sensuous world of souls and bodies. Humanism, secularism, and all related forms of progressive modernity are all covert forms of such monotheism with human identity, the spirit of "I am," taking center stage in ever more condensed form ensnaring humanity always deeper into a cosmic prison of isolation and exile. False promises of a transcendental paradisical eternity of the person or manic nihilism and secularism have provided humanity with the abstract structure of a skeletal logocentric cosmos, which must be defended against the forces of the unconscious, irrational or daemonic. A cosmos ordered vertically, according to ideal and abstract laws originating in transcendence, must be always at odds with a Kosmos of cyclical time and space structured only by the erotic interplay of ensouled polarities within an all-encompassing maternal Urgrund. For the former, paternal cosmos, the daemonic forces represent Chaos, always attempting to intrude into their hierarchical, artificial order. By contrast, in the Kosmic Gnostic perspective, Chaos is the necessary complement of Kosmos, as Chaos is the Mater-to-be who births Kosmos by revealing her secrets in the ceaseless mating of polarities. It must have become clear by now, that the Kosmic Gnosis is fundamentally opposed to cosmos, is essentially an anti-cosmic current, not because it champions any intrusion of transcendence into the cosmos but because it knows of an acausal Kosmos lurking beneath the surface of the skeletal spirit-ruled cosmos.[1]

We should understand Leonard and other cultural iterations of the Black Man as localized daemonic expressions of the emissary, the daemonic power which serves as a gateway into the maternal daemonic Kosmos. Leonard then is the initiator of the primordial way, pointing towards the path leading into the "Open," the wilderness found within the cracks of linear time. We are led out of the metaphysical insulation and a life ruled by a will to power and domination. Our exile in an anthropomorphic world "made in our image," which consumes nature and the Other as object and "standing reserve," comes to an end when we finally return into our own nature, not as a static I, but as a Kosmic event and discloser of life through organic reciprocal relationships with the daemonic atmospheres of the world. It is in this Open, where uncanniness meets serenity, that Leonard presides over the sabbatic festival. The Sabbath is the individual and communal celebration of the Kosmic mysteries, the occasion on which the primordial relations are being reconfirmed. Only then one of the mottos of our magical Society is being fulfilled: "The deeds of the Day must give way to the Wonders of the Night."

Darragh Mason: *The Dark Man in my research demonstrates an initiatory aspect. If he appears or speaks to you in one of his forms, it is a call to witchcraft or mystic inspiration. Does the same hold true for ML?*

David Beth: *I believe this can very well be the case. Although today where true mystical or magical contact is very rare—more often than not what people experience is their own wishful thinking and projection which then is mirrored back to them in "visions" or "dreams," etc.—we have to be careful in accepting any and all claims. But if the Dark Man truly begins to make his presence felt, I think it is important to listen to his whispers. Ignoring his call may lead to negative consequences as his daemonic intrusion may cause an unbalanced psyche and life. In Vodou, when a spirit continuously appears to an individual, such a person usually would then consult a priest or priestess in order to divine the message or demand the spirit has. I would suggest the same to a person who truly is haunted by the Dark Man: consult an authority on the matter to divine a course of action. Of course in the West, most people usually reject any teacher figures or authorities in favor of a self-declared initiatic status, self-study, etc. This is unsurprising given the spiritual insulation of the modern human and the rarity of true spiritual contact. The Gods have fled the logocentric universe as Ludwig Klages, Martin Heidegger knew, and instead the world of the esoteric marketplace is now filled with "phantoms" or Jungian archetypes. But true contact remains possible in special cases, of course; and when the pathic soul encounters the Black Man in his ferocious vitality, the spiritual specialist remains an indispensable figure to assist in grounding and orienting this experience.*

Darragh Mason: *How does ML provide the magical focal point of your occult society?*

David Beth: *Leonard is the initiating daemon who opens the pathways for the Night Watch into the realities of the pan-daemonic Kosmos, the mysteries of the Son/Sol Niger and Chaos-cum-Mater.*

Darragh Mason: *In our correspondence you mentioned the Master Leonard also manifests in your associations with Haitian Vodou. Can you explain this? Is it different from how he manifests for the Leonard Society (assuming he does)? My thinking is this is a magickal current of huge significance that has always been with witches and storytellers in some form or another.*

David Beth: *In Haitian Vodou I have encountered a spirit called Mèt Leonard. He is a djab, a ferocious, hot spirit, and he manifests in the work of my secret society, the Societe Vodou Gnostique (SVG). I personally feel this spirit comes from the same esoteric space which presences the Master Leonard of the Night Watch, and so I believe they are magically related. The Mèt Leonard is a unique "pwen," a magical point, a focus of magical and spiritual energy and provides the SVG with special knowledge and magical power. There are differences in the Vodou rite and the Night Watch in regards to how the spirit is being fed, and also the modus operandi of magical interaction is different.*

I would agree with you in that the magical current of the Black Man is of great importance, especially in regards to magical empowerments, and guiding individuals and communities into communion with the lost Kosmos of daemonic images.

Darragh Mason: *Can you unpack the relationship between the Black Man and the Goat of Mendes?*

David Beth: *Rather than answering this question myself, I would like to quote my fellow initiate Dr. Tomas Vincente (pseudonym). He is a professor of ancient religions and authored a book for Theion Publishing, The Faceless*

God, *in which he masterfully explores this question in relation to the underworld cult of Osiris and later European witchlore.*

> The goat of Mendes was a Greek interpretation of the Egyptian ram of Mendes, Banebdjedet, a form of Osiris (the original Black god) in his netherworld aspect, as the sun-at-night. The Ram was associated with fertility, and thus with the creative potency of the Black Sun. It was Eliphas Levi in the 19th century who revived (and to a large extent reinvented) the lore of the Goat of Mendes, linking the image with his rendering of "Baphomet," which was based on the iconography of the Devil card of the Marseilles Tarot. The original meaning of the Goat of Mendes, and his linkage with the Osirian netherworld mysteries, were reestablished in my book *The Faceless God*, revealing a hitherto unexplored connection with the lore of witchcraft."[2]

Darragh Mason: *I argue in my book that the Dark Man has two identifiable patterns of "general" interaction with human beings. Firstly, he "inspires" creatives through their daimons, and secondly he makes direct contact with those called to witchcraft. When reading through the note provided on Vincente's book* The Faceless God, *I felt the Black Man as emissary—as Anubis—fell somewhere in these patterns. What are your thoughts?*

David Beth: *First, the Faceless God must be understood as the Son, the inborn secret of Chaos-cum-Mater (of the Kosmos), Osiris in the netherworld, manifesting the mysteries of the Sun at Midnight, the Sol Niger. The Son who has no Father is the guarantor of the maternal pan-daemonic Kosmos. He is its most condensed essence of vitality and Life and as the Black Sun, his telesmatic light suffuses the universe. The Black Man or emissary, in his many cultural guises—e.g., the Egyptian Anubis, Lovecraft's "Nyarlathotep," or Master Leonard—is a daemon particularly suited to open the path, to lead us back into the Open where the pandaemonic life, which is basically an establishing of primordial relations, of affecting and being affected, can come to pass. This is why the Black Man or*

Leonard in our tradition is the master of ceremony at the Sabbath but is not served or worshipped as the essence of the daemonic Kosmos itself—which is the Black Sun/Son. Leonard or the Black Man are the messengers of this (anti-cosmic) Kosmic reality of which the Son is the ultimate symbol and essence. As these emissaries are particular daemonic manifestations of telesmatic vitality, they, like all life of the entire Kosmos of daemonic souls, participate in the essence of the Son who is the secret of the Mother.

Allow me to quote my friend Tomas Vincente again, with whom I concur:

> I would be inclined to think that contact [with the Son/Sol Niger] is probably never fully direct, since this would instantly annihilate the human person. The problem of course is the hopeless anthropomorphizing of such occult realities and ignorance of their true cosmogonic power and significance. So, I would tend to suppose that contact is always through daimonic mediation of some form. If we look at the recurring patterns of such contacts we notice: Associations with underworld journeys, which signal a subversion of ordinary cognition (sensory distortion and also trickster phenomena); thus also encounters in anomalous states of awareness and especially dream states; and finally highly synchronistic events, marking a realignment of the psyche with its source. The witchcraft testimonials are interesting in this regard. Of course we have to account for demonological overlays, i.e. diabolical representations of witchcraft as anti-Christianity, and confessions extracted through coercion. It's tricky to use this material as evidence. But it is tempting to wonder whether the constant references to inversion or subversion of Christian rituals might be distorted records of such underworld experiences. In ancient cultures, Egypt, e.g., the underworld, is an upside-down world, a mirror world.[3]

Darragh Mason: *There is a highly charged sexual nature to the Dark Man in* *the historical records and some contemporary accounts. Is this the case in your traditions?*

David Beth: *I personally would rather call it an erotic nature, as his daemonic force, as well as the kosmic reality—which he makes accessible to us— is inextricably bound to an elemental and cosmogonic Eros.* This Eros, in opposition to the logos which orders the skeletal universe of the spirit hierarchically, can be understood as a rhythmic, pulsing web which pervades the entire Kosmos, binding together in ecstasy the daemonic forces, the poles of the world, longing for mating. In this erotic play, no pole is obliterated or consumed by the other but pole gazes at pole and from this encounter the world renews itself at every moment. Of course, rituals of an erotic-gnostic or sexo-magical nature, when born from the above understanding of the reality of the world, can be of great aid in reclaiming one's own daemonic nature and manifesting its ecstatic essence.*

Darragh Mason: *In my personal case, there seems to be a connection with the Dark Man and my paternal line. I don't know for sure, but I believe one of my ancestors initiated contact or gained the Dark Man's interest in some way. Does this type of situation occur with ML in your traditions?*

David Beth: *I believe the particular essence of the Black Man as emissary of a radically different world experience seeks out or naturally impacts certain individuals who still have a more pathic ability, and thus may hear the fading voices of the fugitive gods. While contact with the Black Man or any true daemonic power can never be forced by the "will" (as it is the willful attempt at apprehension which drives the gods away and which is, of course, the reason why most claims at spiritual contact in the modern West are fraudulent or delusional), his arrival can be prepared for. Relations with the Black Man are reciprocal, which means that only when we allow him to remain in his own essence while abiding in ours, without the need for appropriation, will he be able to make meaningful contact.*

---

*We strongly suggest the study of the most eminent treatise on the elemental Eros and its associated ecstasies: Ludwig Klages's *Of Cosmogonic Eros*, Theion Publishing, 2022.

15
Hearing His Song

Pleased to meet you
Hope you guess my name
But what's puzzling you
Is the nature of my game
            "Sympathy for the Devil"
            by the Rolling Stones

In November 2020 I had a vision. It was like nothing I had experienced before. I was mid-meditation when I saw a wall of fire and a single burning eye staring at me. I've never had a challenge with visualization—it's always come relatively easily to me—but this was different. It was vivid, completely immersive, and awe-inspiring. It had color and textures I felt I could reach out and touch. I could feel the heat of the flames on my skin and hear the roar and crackle of the fire. The pupil of the burning eye morphed into a large, muscular figure, silhouetted jet black against the fire. The figure was tall with wavy hair that fell just above the shoulder. The figure unfurled huge black wings and addressed me. An image of the sculpture *Le Génie du Mal* by Guillaume Geefs flashed in my mind's eye followed by the sigil of Lucifer. In one swift movement, the dark angel took off vertically. As it did, I felt like I was rushing up with it. The sensation was like ascending in a fast elevator. I was left frightened and confused and immediately stopped all magical practice.

It would be several months before I could speak about what

happened. The event was like the midday sun: I knew it was there, I could feel its heat, but I couldn't look directly at it. On reflection, what scared me the most was that I could neither deny nor rationalize what I had seen. As a travel photographer I've had experiences that challenged my worldview. They were frightening and strange, but they were easier to process. My research into the esoteric had given context to me that was helpful in understanding what I had experienced previously.

This was different. I didn't require context for me to know something otherworldly had happened. Worse still, it happened in my home. I had not stepped into the territory of the other as I had on previous occasions. Every fiber in my being knew something profound had happened, and I couldn't deal with it.

Months later I opened up to a good friend during a tarot reading. She listened while I went over what happened, and directed me to a friend of hers who has a significant psychic gift. Not long after I sat down for my first online session with Michelle DeVrieze in what would become a monthly meeting. We worked through what had happened. The journey was profound and life changing. All semblance of doubt I had in the reality of the spirit world left me. In the course of our sessions, I would come to understand that the Dark Man had always been with me and had left clues in my childhood, which would come to make sense some thirty-five years later.

Through working with Michelle, I learned that this relationship came down my patriarchal line; that a witch ancestor had an interaction with the Dark Man and, several centuries later, I was untangling the generational fallout. In our sessions Michelle would receive spirit communications. She was accustomed to this and would regularly stop talking midsentence to listen as her spirits would interject into our conversation. These psychic interjections often accurately recount information personal to me that she had no way of knowing. In time, I would become more familiar with what was external to me in terms of these revelations. I came to recognize what was "me" and was "other." The external communication was not always auditory; it often took the form of images. Later, as my research into this book developed, the external also took the form of inspiration and subtle direction to source material.

I was experiencing two types of spirit contact from two entangled sources. First, there were auditory and intense visionary experiences, which were more personal and to the point. These were from *him*. There would be the type of vision I've described, or I'd hear a clear and distinct voice—as Orion Foxwood described. I would often feel a presence when he was with me and see an impression of him in one of his forms in my mind. Sometimes this would be the angelic form; other times it would be a blacker than black, nine-foot humanoid form. Sometimes, in his face, there were stars and moving galaxies in place of features, just as in the story of the child Krishna where his mother, Yashoda, sees the entire universe in his mouth. While these forms were overwhelming at times, it's hard to convey the sense of peace I felt when he was near. I knew I was watched over.

Second, there was the intuitive daimonic communication. Here I was directed to source material and drip-fed concepts. I would be led by my research to a certain text only to find I had purchased it some years before, placed it on a bookshelf, and forgot it.

These instances begged the question of how long had I been led around by the nose by my daimon? The most startling of these occurrences happened while working with Michelle, whose very presence, I suspected, thinned the veil. We had been working together for six months or so and were discussing my initial vision when I recalled a small painting from my parents' home that had a startling similarity to what I had seen. No larger than a sheet of paper in a frame, the painting depicted a simple black silhouetted humanoid figure with wings spread against a shimmering background of peach and lilac flame. A gift from a family friend, I recalled noticing it twelve years earlier, as it was completely incongruous among the family photos. It was remarkably close to what I had seen in my vision. Intuitively I felt that the painting had been meant for me for the exact purpose of realizing the Dark Man had been preparing me for years for this reckoning. The painting would become my central altar piece.

By the end of 2021, I had two writing projects incubating. One was a collection of essays on my various esoteric experiences as a travel and documentary photographer; the other was, well, you're reading it. He was quite insistent as to which project I would pursue. At one stage procrastination and overthinking had ground the work to a halt, and I was told in meditation to *get the fuck on with it*. This language was jarring but it would become recognizable as his voice. The devil, it turns out, has a great sense of humor. But I had a lingering fear that I'd be the punchline somewhere down the road. He is the trickster, after all. Those who worked with him in the past were known as cunning folk for a reason, in that they could work with him and not get eaten. They understood where they were on the food chain. The spirit I was in communication with was not the Christian concept of the Devil as the source and embodiment of the world's evil. Intellectually, I could separate *him* from the Church's propaganda. But in quiet moments of reflection, that separation was not so easy, and I struggled with fearful thoughts as to the nature of what I was working with. The imprints of my Catholic upbringing were deeply rooted in my psyche. And yet I felt I've been protected and supported by *him* throughout my life. This could all be dismissed as my unverified personal gnosis, or UPG as the kids say—I understand that—but as I discovered, there were many others who'd had similar experiences, and when you gnosis, you gnosis.

In tandem, Elise Oursa, Shullie H. Porter, and I had been comparing notes on our recent experiences. Things were escalating and we agreed it was time to do a ritual together to get some answers. Shullie and Elise were planning on attending a week-long artists' retreat in Dartmoor in the southwest of England. Elise suggested I join them for the tail end days of their retreat where, together, we would perform the ritual. We spent Friday evening sitting around a roaring campfire. The night sky was clear and teeming with stars and the milky way shone above us. Warmed by the fire, a bellyful of red wine, and the sweet smell of wood smoke, I stared at the majesty of the night sky.

I often spend time in my garden at night. I'm lucky to live in a relatively rural town with limited light pollution. To be outside in genuine darkness is an experience that many in the West have, sadly, never had. Our world is constantly illuminated with the artificial blue light of our devices and computer screens, blinding us to the world around us—it's difficult to avoid this in the modern world. We view our entire lives through the aperture of our phone screens. It's a compulsion I struggle with every day, but I am aware of how much it takes from me. Turn off the devices and the lights and, in time, you will find life in the darkness and it will find you. In my garden at night, I would have impressions of his presence. My hair would be touched and I would hear my name whispered from the shadows. Unsurprisingly, one of the communications I had from him was to limit my time online and to delete certain social media platforms, which is excellent advice whether it comes from the Devil or not. As Peter Grey and Alkistis Dimech explained, this "is the voice of the land," and protracted time spent in digital worlds will prevent you from hearing it clearly.

One by one the others left their seats by the fireside until just a few of us remained.

"He's over there, watching us," Shullie said matter of factly, pointing into the dark fields beyond the light of the fire. Not long after, I retired for the night and slept reasonably well, despite knowing what the following day held in store for me.

The next morning, we drove down the narrow Devonshire lanes with their towering hedgerows to a nearby ancient church. Situated in a picturesque village, the church was circled by an overgrown graveyard with long grass and wildflowers. It didn't look disheveled or unloved, just wild. As I completed a clockwise circle of the building, I found a single black crow's feather, and then another followed by yet another. As I picked up the third feather, I heard the voice say, "One for each participant."

We spent the rest of the day exploring locations around north Dartmoor. Elise and I spent the morning drawing the ancient stones of the Scorhill stone circle. Deciding that Scorhill would be our location for the ritual later that night, we returned to our campsite and worked through our plans for the midnight ritual. Shullie would call Hecate first as protection, and she prepared offerings of eggs, cake, and honey. I would call the Dark Man using a segment of a spell from Gemma Gary's *The Devil's Dozen*. Elise would use a Typhonian call from the *Papyri Graecae Magicae*. We had been brought together by him, so our discussion around what we wanted to get from him was necessary for some clarity. Elise proposed we ask questions to aid future work: What did he want from us? How would we recognize him? And what should we call him?

Just before midnight we drove to the stone circle. I was silent for most of the drive. As we got closer, it was clear there was a thick mist low on the moor. My nerves were kicking in and I felt out of my depth. We parked and Elise turned to me, "What are we doing, Darragh?"

"I don't know," I replied.

Across the stile was the moor. The mist and wind were worse than I expected, and visibility was poor. Between the danger of getting lost on the moor and my apprehension of what we were going to do, I genuinely contemplated just doing the ritual in the empty parking area. We agreed that going all the way to the stone circle would be foolish. With zero phone coverage and only a few meters of visibility, it was asking for trouble. People get lost and die on Dartmoor. We could easily stray from the track and fall prey to all manner of dangers on the moor, physical and otherworldly.

A dry stone wall ran parallel to the track into the moor. Despite the mist, it was just about visible so, keeping it to our right, we went in, stopping where the wall ended. My headlamp made visibility worse with its white light turning the mist into a featureless white wall. I thought of the Ceo draíochta, the magic mist that marked the boundaries between our world and the otherworld.

Switching to red mode, improved visibility, and still within sight of the wall, we found a space circled by some large stones. We cast a circle to protect us. Not just for the ritual, but Shullie could see and hear spirits gathering around us. Facing north toward the wall and the pine trees behind it, we started. Shullie called aloud:

> *IO Hekate!*
> *IO Hekate!*
> *IO Hekate!*
> *She who is who was ever will be.*
> *Alpha and Omega, beginning and end.*
> *She who opens doors and closes them.*
> *Who holds the keys to Eternity.*
> *She who walks before, behind, beside, and within.*
> *Goddess, mother, sister, hear me your Priestess I beseech*
> *   thee.*
> *Protect those who stand within this circle holding up*
> *   your torch to light the way.*
> *Allow the Dark Man to enter and give his message.*
> *Take these offerings as a sign of our gratitude.*

Then it was my turn.

> *Horned One,*
> *We Bid ye come,*
> *Father of Witches all,*
> *By twain-forked staff, by fume and flame*
> *Hearken ye unto our call!*
> *Horned One,*
> *We bid ye come,*
> *Father of the Witches all.*

My nervousness got the better of me, so I didn't read aloud confidently. Perhaps sensing this, my companions joined me as we read again in chorus, calling out loud into the darkness. As we finished, we heard a child cry as the thick curtains of mist intermittently blocked our view. I called to him to accept my offering of libation and poured a bottle of red wine onto the moor. Elise was next. Reciting from memory she said aloud in ancient Greek her call to Typhon, finishing with an offering of wine and brandy. We waited. A light appeared to the north between the tree branches, and we watched as it grew and shrank, wondering if it was a star, low in the sky, or perhaps a torch in the distance. The wind died down abruptly and the mist momentarily cleared. Something in the air changed. There was absolute silence. He was here. I watched the trees, part of me expecting him to step out of the shadows as he did for Isobel Gowdie. Emphasizing there were no deals or pacts to be made, we asked our questions.

"What should we call you?" Shullie asked aloud.

I heard the familiar man's voice in my head whisper, "Lucifer." Shullie confirmed the same.

"How will we know you?"

"The Dark, darkness, shining one." The voice said each word clearly and slowly.

"What do you want from me?" I asked.

The voice responded with a single word, in the terse manner I was accustomed to: "Write."

Each of us received our own answer to the last question. I share mine because you hold the result in your hands.

It was over. Thanking him, we gathered our belongings and started closing down the circle. On the first pass, Shullie mentioned there were more spirits all around us being held back by the circle.

"Fuck off," she said, dismissing them. We circled around a second time, and something pulled her off balance.

"FUCK OFF," she shouted into the darkness. On the third and final pass, the spirits dragged her out of the ritual space and into the mist. Before I had grasped what was happening, Elise pulled Shullie back to us and screamed into the darkness:

"AKTIOPHIS ERESCHEKIGAL NEBOUTOSOALETH!"

Whatever was harassing Shullie backed off immediately, and we quickly made our way back to the car. "I can feel something on my arm," said Elise as she struggled with her keys. Something had attached itself to her on the moor. When we got back to our lodgings, she scrubbed her arm with salt and water, and the sensation left. We sat together and had a glass of wine and some chocolate to ground us. To my surprise, it was only 12:45 a.m. It felt a hell of a lot later. I slept poorly in my tent that night, in part because it was no larger than a coffin but mostly because of the night's events. I was grateful for the company of my witch sisters. This was not an undertaking I could have managed on my own. Nor would I have dared to. My mettle had been well and truly tested.

"Write," he told me. This wasn't entirely a surprise. I had been working on the proposal for this book at the time. What was a surprise was the sequence of events that meant two days after the ritual, I took a call from my future publisher, and not long after that I had a contract and a deadline. The Lord of the Crossroads had cleared the way; it was time for me to write. I've done as I was asked.

If you need more, you know where to find him.

Good luck.

Notes

FOREWORD

1. Wilby, *Visions of Isobel Gowdie.*
2. Procopius, "Gothic War," 48–58.
3. Ginzburg, *Ecstasies.*
4. Turner, et al., *Experiencing Ritual.*
5. Grindal, "Into the Heart."
6. Deren, *Divine Horsemen.*
7. Turner, "Reality of Spirits."
8. Thurnell-Read, *Geopathic Stress.*
9. Wilby, *Visions of Isobel Gowdie*, 19.

CHAPTER 1. FIRE IN THE BLOOD

1. "Miscellaneous Extracts," p. 1.
2. Williams, "Devil Looking Down."
3. Moriarty, *Invoking Ireland*, 40.
4. Plato, *Apology*, 115.
5. Jung, *Letters*, 532.
6. Jaffé, *Jung's Last Years*, 141.
7. Jung, *Collected Works*, 115–116.
8. Dylan, Interview.
9. Auryn, "Witch Blood."
10. Lebling, *Legends*, 167–168.
11. Hanegraaff and Kripal, *Hidden Intercourse*, 53–56, 58.

12. Stuart, *Miscellany*, 119.

13. Lenihan and Green, *Meeting the Other Crowd*, 264.

14. Artisson, *Horn of Evenwood*, 80.

CHAPTER 2. THE BLACK MAGICIAN OF THE MEN OF GOD

1. Beck, *Goddesses in Celtic Religion*, 75.

2. Beck, *Goddesses in Celtic Religion*, 75.

3. Gwynn, *Metrical Dindshenchas*, Part 2, 66.

4. Wilby, *Visions of Isobel Gowdie*, 39.

5. Rolleston, *Celtic Myths and Legends*, 266–268, 270.

6. Stephens, *Irish Fairy Tales*, 104–107.

7. Ó hÓgáin, *Lore of Ireland*, 179.

8. Gray, *Cath Maige Tuired*, 25.

9. "Text and Translation," 27–29.

10. Taylor, "Letter Dated 1577," 60.

11. Platt, *Adam and Eve*, 37.

12. Platt, *Adam and Eve*, 53.

CHAPTER 3. OISÍN, THE LITTLE FAWN

1. Stephens, *Irish Fairy Tales*, 120.

2. Genesis 1:2 (King James Version of the Bible).

3. "Ossian Legendary Gaelic Poet."

4. "Ossian's Dream."

5. Rolleston, *Celtic Myths and Legends*, 270–271.

6. Rolleston, *Celtic Myths and Legends*, 272.

7. Gregory, *Irish Mythology*, 296.

8. Gregory, *Irish Mythology*, 300.

9. MacNeill, *Festival of Lughnasa*, 416.

10. Dames, *Merlin and Wales*, 26–27.

CHAPTER 4. THE DARK INTERCEPTOR

1. "Definitely not a Helping Hand."

2. Artisson, *Horn of Evenwood*, 85.

3. Walsh, "Ghost Story."

4. Wilde, *Ancient Legends*, 264.

5. Wilde, *Ancient Legends*, 260.

6. "Maya Indian Philosophy."

CHAPTER 5. TRICKY TRICKSTER, CULTURE CHANGER

1. Harpur, *Daimonic Reality*, 167.

2. Queenan, *Reflections*, 93.

3. Queenan, *Reflections*, 93.

4. Waller, "Forgotten Plague," 624–645.

5. "Herring, "Monsters."

6. Reed, "Spring-Heeled Jack."

7. Reed, "Spring-Heeled Jack."

8. Dash, "Spring-Heeled Jack."

9. May, "Paranormal Experts."

10. Anne4884, "Black Figure on the Road."

11. Crowley, *Equinox of the Gods*, 117.

12. Crowley, *Equinox of the Gods*, 118.

13. Crowley, *Equinox of the Gods*, 118.

14. Crowley, *Magick in Theory*, 193.

15. "Atomic Bombings."

16. Mirabai, "I saw witchcraft tonight."

CHAPTER 6. THE DARK WOMB AND REWILDING THE SOUL

1. Hutton, *Witches*, 34.

2. Clottes, *Cave Art*, 129.

3. Rolleston, *Celtic Myths and Legends*, 130.

4. Gwynn, *Metrical Dindshenchas*, Part 3, 31.

5. Gwynn, *Metrical Dindshenchas*, Part 3, 293.

6. Stephens, *Irish Fairy Tales*, 26.

7. Dames, *Mythic Ireland*, 190.

8. Stephens, *Irish Fairy Tales*, 66.

9. Stephens, *Irish Fairy Tales*, 66.

CHAPTER 7. CONFESSIONS OF WITCHES

1. Brown, "Religion and Society," 81.
2. Grey, *Apocalyptic Witchcraft*, 16.
3. Goodare, et al., *Survey of Scottish Witchcraft*.
4. Goodare, et al., *Survey of Scottish Witchcraft*.
5. Goodare, et al., *Survey of Scottish Witchcraft*.
6. Goodare, et al., *Survey of Scottish Witchcraft*.
7. Goodare, et al., *Survey of Scottish Witchcraft*.
8. Goodare, et al., *Survey of Scottish Witchcraft*.
9. Goodare, et al., *Survey of Scottish Witchcraft*.
10. Wilby, *Visions of Isobel Gowdie*, 37, 39.
11. Wilby, *Visions of Isobel Gowdie*, 37, 39.
12. Cutchin, Ecology of Souls, Volume 1, 176.
13. Wilby, *Visions of Isobel Gowdie*, 46–47.
14. Wilby, *Visions of Isobel Gowdie*, 49.
15. Collin de Plancy, *Dictionnaire Infernal*.
16. Levi, *Dogme et Rituel*, 84.
17. Wilby, *Visions of Isobel Gowdie*, 39–40.
18. Wilby, *Visions of Isobel Gowdie*, 39–40.
19. Wilby, *Visions of Isobel Gowdie*, 39–40.
20. Wilby, *Visions of Isobel Gowdie*, 43.
21. Wilby, *Visions of Isobel Gowdie*, 43.
22. Artisson, *Horn of Evenwood*, 78.
23. Artisson, *Horn of Evenwood*, 79.

CHAPTER 9. JESSICA MITCHELL, GLASTONBURY TOR

1. Ferguson, "British Race," 194.

CHAPTER 14. DAVID BETH ON MASTER LEONARD

1. Beth, "Clavis Saturni," 14ff.
2. Tomas Vincente, personal communication.
3. Tomas Vincente, personal communication.

Bibliography

Anne4884 (username). "The Black Figure on the Road." Accessed September 20, 2022. Available online on the *Your Ghost Stories* website.

Artisson, Robin. *The Horn of Evenwood*. Los Angeles: Pendriag Publishing, 2007.

Asatrian, Garnik S., and Victoria Arakelova. *The Religion of the Peacock Angel: The Yezidis and Their Spirit World*. New York: Routledge, 2014.

"Atomic Bombings of Hiroshima and Nagasaki." NBC News Archives, accessed September 21, 2022, on YouTube.

Auryn, Mat. "Witch Blood: The Magickal Orientation." Accessed December 28, 2022 on the *For Puck's Sake* blog on the Patheos website.

Beck, Noémie, *Goddesses in Celtic Religion: Cult and Mythology: A Comparative Study of Ancient Ireland, Britain and Gaul*. PhD dissertation, Université Lumière Lyon 2, 2009.

Beth, David. "Clavis Saturni: A Kosmic Heresy," in Moros, Arthur. *The Cult of the Black Cube*. Munich: Theion Publishing, 2022.

Brown, S. J. "Religion and society to c. 1900," *The Oxford Handbook of Modern Scottish History*. Oxford: Oxford University Press, 2012.

Chumbley, Andrew D. *QUTUB, also called The Point*. Hercules, CA.: Xoanon Publishers, 1995.

Clottes, Jean. *Cave Art*. London: Phaidon Press, 2010.

Collin de Plancy, Jacques. "Dictionnaire Infernal." Accessed December 4, 2022. Available online on the Academia.edu website.

Crowley, Aleister. *The Equinox of the Gods*. Leeds: Celephaïs Press, 2004.

Crowley, Aleister. *Magick in Theory and Practice*. Paris: Lecram Press, 1924.

Cutchin, Joshua. *Ecology of Souls: A New Mythology of Death & the Paranormal*, Volume One. Horse & Barrel Press, 2022.

Dames, Michael. *Merlin and Wales: A Magician's Landscape*. London: Thames and Hudson, 2002.

Dames, Michael. *Mythic Ireland*. London: Thames and Hudson, 1992.

Dash, Mike, "Spring-heeled Jack to Victorian Bugaboo from Suburban Ghost." *Fortean Studies* 3 (1996): 7–125. Available online on the Mike Dash website.

"Definitely not a Helping Hand . . . ," BBC Devon. Accessed September 5, 2022. Available online on the BBC UK website.

Deren, Maya. *Divine Horsemen: Living Gods of Haiti*. Kingston, NY.: McPherson, 1985.

Dylan, Bob, interview by Ed Bradley. *60 Minutes*. CBS, December 6, 2004. Available online on YouTube.

Evans, J. Gwenogvryn, ed. *The Black Book of Carmarthen*. Pwllheli, 1907.

Ferguson, James, "The British Race and Kingdom in Scotland," *The Celtic Review, Volume 8 May 1912–May 1913,* 1913.

Garner, Alan. *The Guizer*. London: Fontana Lions, 1980.

Gary, Gemma. *The Devil's Dozen Thirteen Craft Rites of the Old One*. London: Troy Books, 2015.

Ginzburg, Carlo. Ecstasies: *Deciphering the Witches' Sabbath*. New York: Pantheon, 1991.

Goodare, Julian, Lauren Martin, Joyce Miller, and Louise Yeoman. *The Survey of Scottish Witchcraft*. Scottish History. January 2003. Available online on the University of Edinburgh's School of History, Classics and Archaeology website.

Gray, A. Elizabeth, ed. *Cath Maige Tuired: The Second Battle of Mag Tuired*. Kildare: Irish Text Society, 1982.

Gregory, Lady. *Lady Gregory's Complete Irish Mythology*. London: Bounty Books, 2006.

Grey, Peter. *Apocalyptic Witchcraft*. London: Scarlet Imprint, 2013.

Grey, Peter. *Lucifer: Princeps*. London: Scarlet Imprint, 2015.

Grey, Peter. *The Two Antichrists*. London: Scarlet Imprint, 2021.

Grindal, Bruce. "Into the Heart of Sisala Experience: Witnessing Death Divination." *Journal of Anthropological Research* 39, no 1 (1983): 60–80.

Gwynn, Edward, ed. *The Metrical Dindshenchas Part 2, Royal Irish Academy Todd Lecture Series*. Dublin: Hodges, Figgis, 1906.

Gwynn, Edward, ed. *The Metrical Dindshenchas Part 3, Royal Irish Academy Todd Lecture Series*. Dublin: Hodges, Figgis, 1913.

Hanegraaff, Wouter J., and Jeffery Kripal. *Hidden Intercourse: Eros and Sexuality in the History of Western Esotericism*. Leiden: Brill, 2008.

Harpur, Patrick. *Daimonic Reality: A Field Guide to the Otherworld*. Ravensdale, WA: Pine Winds Press, 2003.

Herring, Richard. "Monsters Are a Product of the Madness of City Life," *Metro*. Accessed September 21, 2022. Available online on the *Metro* website.

Hutton, Ronald. *Witches, Druids, and King Arthur*. London: Hambledon and London, 2003.

Hyde, Lewis. *Trickster Makes This World: How Disruptive Imagination Creates Culture*. Edinburgh: Canongate Books, 2008.

Jaffé, Aniela. *Jung's Last Years*. Dallas: Spring Publications, 1984.

Jung, C. G. *C. J. Letters Vol. II, 1951–1961*. Gerhard Adler and Aniela Jaffé eds. Hove: Routledge, 1990.

Jung, C. G. *The collected works of C. G. Jung, vol 15: The spirit in man, art, and literature*. Princeton: Princeton University Press, 1978.

Kirk, Robert. *The Secret Commonwealth of Elves, Fauns and Fairies*. New York: Dover Publications, 2008.

Klages, Ludwig. *Of Cosmogonic Eros*. Munich: Theion Publishing, 2019.

Kruse, John. *British Fairies*. Somerset: Green Magic, 2017.

Lebling, Robert. *Legends of the Fire Spirits: Jinn and Genies from Arabia to Zanzibar*. London: I. B. Tauris, 2014.

Lenihan, Eddie, and Carolyn Eve Green. *Meeting the Other Crowd: The Fairy Stories of Hidden Ireland*. Dublin: Gill Books, 2003.

Levi, Eliphas. *Dogme et Rituel de la Haute Magie Part II: The Ritual of Transcendental Magic*. A. E. Waite, trans. Benjamin Rowe, 2002.

MacNeill, Máire. *The Festival of Lughnasa: A Study of the Survival of the Celtic Festival of the Beginning of Harvest*. London: Oxford University Press, 1982.

May, L. "Terrified Banstead family confronted by 'dark figure' on bypass," *Sutton & Croydon Guardian*, February 23, 2012. Available online on the *Your Local Guardian* website.

May, Lauren. "Paranormal Experts Weigh in on Dark Figure Mystery," *Sutton and Croydon Guardian*. Accessed September 19, 2022. Available online on the *Your Local Guardian* website.

"Maya Indian Philosophy." Accessed September 9, 2022. Available online on the *Britannica* website.

Mirabai, "O I saw witchcraft tonight," *Ecstatic Poems*. English version by Robert Bly and Jane Hirshfield. Boston, MA: Beacon Press, 2004.

Miscellaneous Extracts. *Bell's Life in Sydney and Sporting Reviewer*, May 26, 1855, p. 1. accessed August 10, 2022. Available online on the trove.nla.gov .au website.

Moriarty, John. *Invoking Ireland: Ailiu Iath n-Herend*. Dublin: The Lilliput Press, 2019.

Morgan, Lee. *Sounds of Infinity*. Newport, RI: The Witches' Almanac, 2019.

Ó hÓgáin, Dáithí. *The Lore of Ireland: An Encyclopaedia of Myth, Legend and Romance*. Cork: Collins Press, 2006.

"Ossian's Dream (Le Songe D'Ossian)." Accessed August 14, 2022. Available online on the Napoleon.org website.

"Ossian Legendary Gaelic Poet." Accessed August 10, 2022. Available online on the *Britannica* website.

Pickering, Andrew. *The Witches of Selwood: Witchcraft Belief and Accusation in Seventeenth-Century Somerset*. Gloucester: Hobnob Press, 2021.

Plato: Euthyphro. Apology. Crito. Phaedo. Phaedrus. Harold North Fowler, trans. Cambridge, MA: Harvard University Press, 2005.

Platt, Rutherford H. *The First Book of Adam and Eve*. Global Grey Book, 2022.

Procopius. "Gothic War." In *History of the Wars*, Volume V: Books 7.36–8. Translated by H. B. Dewing. Loeb Classical Library 217. Cambridge, MA: Harvard University Press, 1928.

Queenan, Bernard. "The Evolution of the Pied Piper," in Butler, Francelia, and Richard Rotert eds. *Reflections on Literature for Children*. Hamden, CT: Library Professional Publications, 1984.

Reed, Peter. "Spring-Heeled Jack," Epsom & Ewell History Explorer. Accessed September 20, 2022. Available online on the eehe.org website.

Rolleston, T. W. *Celtic Myths and Legends*. London: Studio Editions, 1995.

Rose, Megan, PhD. *Spirit Marriage: Intimate Relationships with Otherworldly Beings*. Rochester, VT: Bear & Company, 2022.

Shah, Idries. *The Sufis*. London: A Star Book, 1977.

Stephens, James. *Irish Fairy Tales*. Istanbul: e-Kitap Projesi, 2019.

Stuart J., ed. "Trials for Witchcraft," *The Miscellany of the Spalding Club*, Volume 1. Aberdeen: Spalding Club, 1841.

"The Survey of Scottish Witchcraft." Accessed November 1, 2022. Available online on the University of Edinburgh's School of History, Classics and Archaeology website.

Taylor, E. G. R. "A letter dated 1577 from Mercator to John Dee," *Imago Mundi: The International Journal for the History of Cartography* 13 no. 1, (1956), 60.

"Text and Translation of the Legends of the Original Chart of the World by Gerhard Mercator, Issued in 1569." *The International Hydrographic Review* 9 no. 2, (1932), 27–29.

Thurnell-Read, J. *Geopathic Stress: How Earth Energies Affect Our Lives.* Gloucester: Element Books, 1996.

Turner, Edith, William Blodgett, Singleton Kahona, and Fideli Benwa. *Experiencing Ritual: A New Interpretation of African Healing.* Philadelphia: University of Pennsylvania Press, 1992.

Turner, Edith. "The Reality of Spirits." *Shamanism* 10, no. 1 (1997).

Waller, John, "A Forgotten Plague: Making Sense of Dancing Mania," *The Lancet*, 373:9664, (2009).

Walsh, Edward. "A Ghost Story." Accessed September 3, 2022. Available online on the Duchas.ie website.

Wells, Deborah. *The Dark Man.* Winchester: O-Books, 2010.

Wilde, Lady Jane Francesca Agnes. *Ancient Legends of Ireland: Mystic Charms & Superstitions of Ireland with Sketches of the Irish Past.* Galway: O'Gorman, 1971.

Wilby, Emily. *Cunning-Folk and Familiar Spirits: Shamanistic Visionary Traditions in Early Modern British Witchcraft and Magic.* Eastbourne: Sussex Academic Press, 2013.

Wilby, Emily. *The Visions of Isobel Gowdie: Magic, Witchcraft and Dark Shamanism in Seventeenth-Century Scotland.* Eastbourne: Sussex Academic Press, 2013.

Williams, Nino. "Why there's a devil looking down on everyone from the Swansea Quadrant Shopping Centre." Accessed September 19, 2022. Available online on the *Wales Online* website.

Index

BOOKS OF RELATED INTEREST

Slavic Witchcraft
Old World Conjuring Spells and Folklore
by Natasha Helvin

Ancestral Slavic Magic
Transcend Family Patterns and Empower Ancestral Connections
by Natasha Helvin

The Path of Elemental Witchcraft
A Wyrd Woman's Book of Shadows
by Salicrow

Tales of Witchcraft and Wonder
The Venomous Maiden and Other Stories of the Supernatural
by Claude Lecouteux and Corinne Lecouteux

Tales and Legends of the Devil
The Many Guises of the Primal Shapeshifter
by Claude Lecouteux and Corinne Lecouteux

Lords of the Left-Hand Path
Forbidden Practices and Spiritual Heresies
by Stephen E. Flowers, Ph.D.

Familiars in Witchcraft
Supernatural Guardians in the Magical Traditions of the World
by Maja D'Aoust

Traditional Brazilian Black Magic
The Secrets of the Kimbanda Magicians
by Diego de Oxóssi
Foreword by Hendrix Silveira

INNER TRADITIONS • BEAR & COMPANY
P.O. Box 388
Rochester, VT 05767
1-800-246-8648
www.InnerTraditions.com

Or contact your local bookseller